WHY VOTE

HOW TO MAKE YOUR VOICE HEARD IN A WORLD OF BROKEN POLITICS

WHY
VOTE

JO PHILLIPS AND DAVID SEYMOUR

Biteback Publishing

First published in Great Britain in 2024 by
Biteback Publishing Ltd, London
Copyright © Jo Phillips and David Seymour 2024

ISBN: 978-1-78590-861-3

10 9 8 7 6 5 4 3 2 1

A CIP catalogue record for this book is available from the British Library.

Set in Minion Pro

Printed and bound in Great Britain by
CPI Group (UK) Ltd, Croydon CR0 4YY

FSC
www.fsc.org
MIX
Paper | Supporting
responsible forestry
FSC® C171272

CONTENTS

FOREWORD

Since we wrote *Why Vote?* ahead of the 2010 election, we've had a referendum that led to Brexit, the Covid-19 pandemic, war in Ukraine and the Middle East, increasing fear over climate emergency as the planet got dangerously hotter, a new monarch and six Prime Ministers. Yes, six. It's as if the world has gone mad – and particularly this country.

But can you do anything about it? This book sets out to show you can. It is for people who are ambivalent about voting, who feel like they don't know enough to make a decision, who simply can't be bothered or are maybe voting for the first time, for people who think all politicians are the same and that voting makes no difference. We hope to persuade you otherwise.

Everyone under the age of thirty-two will know nothing but Conservative governments, except when they were a child. The Conservatives have been in power since 2010, although they formed a coalition government with the Liberal Democrats for the first five years. But, whatever your age, you will have had your life, studies, relationships and maybe even your health upended by Covid. Since Brexit, when the UK left the European Union, you no longer have the same freedom to work, study and travel in other European countries. Freedom to protest peacefully has been curtailed, the cost of further education has deterred some people from going to university and burdened those who do go with a huge debt, while the chances of owning your own home or even finding somewhere to rent are getting slimmer.

Yet if young people turned out to vote in the same numbers that older ones do, Britain might not be suffering as it is and the future, if not completely rosy, might not look so gloomy.

In fairness, not everything that has happened was caused by government or politicians. The war in Ukraine was started by President Putin's invasion, so it is his responsibility alone. The Covid-19 pandemic, which killed almost seven million people worldwide and nearly a quarter of a million in the UK, wasn't caused by politicians – although as you will see in the chapter on Covid, the government could have prevented many of those deaths if it had acted faster and made different decisions. But, some of what has happened is entirely down to politicians who should forever be shamed in a rogues' gallery for destroying the United Kingdom's international reputation. The gap between rich and poor has increased, there are record numbers of people waiting for medical treatment, tens of thousands of families are living in poor housing, raw sewage is being pumped into our seas and rivers and almost everyone except the super wealthy is worried about the cost of living and the future.

The United Kingdom, home of the Mother of Parliaments and admired throughout most of the world for its political stability, seemed to take leave of its senses by calling a national referendum on whether we should remain in the European Union. The result, Brexit, led to a chaotic situation in which the country found itself with six Prime Ministers in seven years. The last two, Liz Truss and Rishi Sunak, were not elected in a general election, but by less than 0.12 per cent of the electorate – by members of the Conservative Party in Truss's case and Tory MPs in Sunak's, which means that more than 99.88 per cent of us are governed by people we never had the chance to vote on. Not terribly democratic, is it?

And if you think that democratic choice means the people's will decides the outcome, think again. Older people are far more likely to vote than the under-thirties, which means that older generations are determining the future of this country: your future is being abandoned into their hands. Turnout at the 2019 general election was around 63 per cent, so more than one in three failed to vote, and of those who did, the biggest age group voting is consistently the over sixty-fives.

If younger people don't vote, then apathy, or despair, have won hands down. Yet people aren't apathetic. They care deeply about climate change, the state of the health service, lack of affordable housing, the cost of living, immigration, education and transport. It is understandable that people feel powerless, particularly after the last few bruising years, and the future is scary. That's why we all need to shape a tomorrow that is better, healthier, fairer and safer. We cannot afford to turn our backs on democracy because the decisions made by governments have far-reaching implications for all of us and for future generations.

Governments make decisions that affect our lives, from where children go to school and how much we pay in taxes, to what hours we work and how much we get paid. They control where and how fast we drive, what and when we can drink in a bar and where new homes can be built. They also decide where and when our armed forces will be sent to war, how the elderly are cared for and whether we can vote at all, as well as countless other issues that shape our present and our future.

People who don't use their vote help to elect governments that don't have the overwhelming support of voters, which is a bit like a football team winning the Premier League with a clutch of offside goals and a few extra players that nobody complained about because they simply couldn't be bothered. Our current system also allows the Prime Minister to call an election when he or she decides, which, to continue the football theme, is like letting one team blow the final whistle when they are winning. No self-respecting football fan would let that happen, so why let it happen to our country?

So there is a lot at stake and you might want to have a say by using your vote: in fact, you really, really *ought* to use your vote, even though the government has introduced rules to make it harder for you: like having to produce specific photo ID before you can do so. Surely that should make you even more determined to exercise the democratic right which past generations fought so hard to win.

CHAPTER 1

A NATION DIVIDED

There is an old saying that you should never discuss religion, politics or sex in polite company, but in the open society that blossomed in the 1960s, nothing was taboo. Healthy debate was considered to be just that: healthy. You might have a heated row but the combatants usually parted on good terms.

Tragically, that changed with Brexit. Britain suddenly became a country divided. Friends, neighbours, even family, found they couldn't discuss certain topics unless they didn't mind becoming involved in a furious row.

It wasn't just on social media that people discovered that what they thought was a simple statement of fact or an opinion would be met with fury, vilification and contempt. Just going to the pub or inviting people round for dinner could become a no-go area, where every step had to be taken gingerly for fear of poking an angry, snarling bear.

And it wasn't only Brexit. The growth of conspiracy theories about climate change and even Covid-19 – yes, there are people who insist it doesn't exist (apparently, those 7 million dead died of natural causes) – can divide long-time friends and ruin family gatherings. This great divide is most obvious in the United States, where some of Donald Trump's more rabid followers are filled with hatred for those who don't hold him in the same regard that they do.

This never used to be the British way of doing things. Discussions, debates and even arguments were conducted in a civilised manner. There might have been no chance of persuading your adversary that you were right, but that didn't mean your disagreement would turn nasty. You parted as friends, often with respect for the other person's opinions, even if you didn't agree with them, but now the mere mention of any of the taboo topics will launch a furious response.

The obvious way to deal with this problem is to know the facts. After all, facts are facts are facts. At least they used to be. Nowadays,though, facts aren't facts for some people. There only needs to be one scientist who doesn't believe in climate change when thousands do, or one economist who thinks Brexit was a good idea which is working when there are thousands who disagree, and that is all the 'proof' they need to confirm their opinions. You will be told: 'Scientists [plural] say there is no such thing as climate change.' So name them, you ask, and the same name will always come up: the same solitary name and no others. The same phenomenon happens with Brexit and the one economist who provides all the 'evidence' that is needed to confirm how brilliantly it is doing.

The consequence is that either you decide it isn't worth trying to persuade the person you are talking to that they are spouting nonsense and so you give up, leaving your adversary with a smug look on their face because they have 'won' and are convinced that their views are correct, or you carry on in an argument that gets more and more heated and more and more unpleasant. This is how the bad guys win.

It is mainly a problem with people who have right-wing views, yet they don't have the monopoly on being massively wrong. Some on the left are convinced that Covid-19 doesn't exist and so believe they don't need to be vaccinated against it, just like the Trumpian fanatics in the States.

In the past, people said they knew something because 'I saw it in the papers'. Now there is an even greater problem because so many newspapers have flipped into eccentricity and extreme views, compounded many times over by being magnified on the internet and certain TV channels – Fox News in the USA and GB News in Britain.

Too often a social gathering becomes a cesspit of angry, spit-flecked rants with finger-jabbing and table-thumping. The chance of them listening to what you say, let alone changing their mind, is remote, but if you don't stand up for what you believe in, you are letting your opponents win by default. Stay calm, put your points across forcefully and give them the real facts. Maybe they won't believe them, but do it anyway. At least you won't have let the dangerous people who threaten our country, and our democracy, go unchallenged.

CHAPTER 2

AND THE RESULT IS... WE'RE OUT

The first results of the Brexit referendum were announced in the early hours of 24 June 2016 and it soon became clear that the nation had voted to leave the European Union. At least, 52 per cent had. The result was not just a shock to Prime Minister David Cameron, Remain campaigners and business, but also to Boris Johnson and Nigel Farage, who had led the Leave campaign without expecting to win. They were stunned when they learned the result. In fact, Farage had gone on television after the polls closed to concede defeat, while Johnson, who was watching the results on TV at his home in north London wearing a Brazil football shirt and shorts, is reported to have said: ' What the hell is happening? … Holy crap, what will we do?'

Cameron immediately resigned as Prime Minister, creating an even bigger problem, as now there was not just no plan, but nobody in charge to work one out. The resulting chaos led to even more chaos, which in turn led to still more chaos. There were a number of knock-on effects which no one had foreseen. These included a succession of Tory leaders and Prime Ministers being picked not by voters, but by a tiny number of party members, mainly white and old and living in the south of England. The Conservative Party, which took pride in presenting a united front to voters while Labour regularly tore itself apart, launched into a vicious civil war.

A growing number of Tory MPs gathered under the banner of an organisation called the European Research Group. In reality, they didn't research anything but were a band of dedicated enemies of anything European. There were enough of them to be able to defeat any proposal the government – *their* government – put forward to reach a deal with the EU. It appeared that the only thing that would satisfy them was a complete break with Europe. Even though most of our trade was with EU countries (because Europe was just 20 miles away across the Channel, unlike, say, America, which is 3,000 miles distant, or Australia, which is more than 9,000 miles away). One MP even announced that he had just discovered, to his surprise, that Britain was particularly reliant on the Dover–Calais crossing for trade. His name was Dominic Raab and he was then the Brexit Secretary before becoming Foreign Secretary.

We will go into more detail about what happened to domestic politics later, but let's concentrate for a moment on what was going on with our relationship with the EU. One of the Brexit campaign's key arguments during the referendum was that, if we left, nothing would change for the worse. We would be free of what they called the shackles of Europe while enjoying our new-found freedom. That was like some-one getting a divorce saying that while it was great being able to go out and have fun like they did before having a partner and children, they would keep their spouse's income, go on living in the family home and driving the family car and see their children whenever they wanted without the problems of taking them to school, looking after them when they were sick and all the other joys of parenthood. Life just ain't like that.

It soon became clear that many of the advantages we had taken for granted when we were in the European Union weren't there anymore. These meant that UK citizens now had to join long, slow queues for passport checks when they arrived in other European countries, whereas before they could just walk in while waving jauntily at customs officers, and businesses now had to fill in huge, lengthy forms when they exported goods to EU countries. The 'bonfire of red tape' that had been promised if Britain left the EU became, in reality, the strangulation of many British businesses by endless kilo-metres of new red tape.

The Brexiteers knew who was to blame. It was the EU of course! As if they had insisted that we should vote to leave and impose the hardest possible deal on ourselves. Most of the fishing industry had voted to leave because they thought that other countries were catching 'our' fish. They now dis-covered that we could catch the fish but that the fish in 'our' waters needed to be sold in the EU because Brits didn't want it, so that became a huge problem.

The farming industry had also supported the Leave campaign because they thought they'd had to do too much paperwork as members of the EU, even though farmers had received generous payments from the European Union's common agricultural policy, so you might think that filling in a few forms once a year wasn't asking too much. As soon as we'd left the EU, farmers discovered that our government had no intention of paying them as much and that there were even more forms to fill in, as well as environmental hoops to jump through.

The ending of freedom of movement, which had allowed people from every EU country to travel to and work in other EU countries, had been a key reason why many voted Leave. They thought these incomers were taking their jobs *and* only coming to Britain to get welfare benefits, not seeming to realise that both could not be true. In fact, neither of those assumptions were – the UK had agreed with the EU that benefits would not be paid to those without a job until people had been here for a couple of years. Above all, it soon became clear that Britain needed workers from other countries for particular jobs. Thousands used to come here to pick crops every year, but now much of the country's harvests rotted in the fields. Thousands of doctors and nurses from European countries had worked in the NHS, which now saw a growing shortage of key medical personnel as the unwanted waved these shores goodbye.

Restaurants, cafes, hotels and even pubs also struggled to find staff to fill the vacancies that had been taken by young

Europeans who often came to Britain for a few years to work and improve their English. Scientists and academics went home too, even those who had been here for years.

But enough of the depressing downside of leaving the European Union. What about the great advantages that the UK got out of Brexit? It soon became common for government ministers, MPs and other Brexiteers to be asked to name one thing that leaving the EU had given us. This was always followed by a long and embarrassing silence. What they eventually came up with was the successful vaccine programme which saw Britons being the first people to be inoculated against Covid-19 and which Brexiteers claimed could not have been done if we had still been in the European Union. This is a good point: except it isn't true. Any EU member state was free to pursue their own vaccine development, as well as participating in the EU-wide programme. In fact, although the UK was the first to start vaccinating, other countries began their vaccination programme only a few days later.

So, were there any other benefits to Brexit? Well, there were the seventy-two trade deals signed with non-European countries. Except that all of these deals had simply rolled over from deals the EU had, so we had enjoyed them before Brexit. Then there were the trade agreements we concluded with Australia and New Zealand in 2022, although over the next fifteen years these will only be worth a tiny amount compared with the value of trade with the EU we have lost and, in any case, they could do serious damage to our farming industry. Even former pro-Brexit Environment Secretary and Farming Minister George Eustice described it as 'not actually a very good deal' and that giving Australia and New Zealand full access to the UK market to sell beef and sheep was one of the worst concessions, and potentially disastrous for UK farming.

CHAPTER 3

ASK A SILLY QUESTION...

One question regularly posed in opinion polls is: what are the most important issues facing voters, their families and the country? Top of the list, or near the top, are usually what you would expect: the cost-of-living, the NHS and housing. The order changes from time to time and sometimes a different issue pops up, yet there was a consistency about what issue was regularly bottom, or very close to the bottom, of the list of concerns: Europe. It bumped along at between 3 and 5 per cent of voters, except when there was a controversy over a particular issue such as the Maastricht treaty or a European election.

But, for that 3 per cent of the population, Europe was THE big issue: an obsession. For some, it was because they passionately believed in European countries working together after the wartime horrors of the first half of the twentieth century. For the others who fell into that tiny minority, Europe was despised and the UK's involvement in the EU was seen as the ultimate betrayal of the British people. We had won

11

the war, after all, and we were better than every other country, as one Tory minister, Gavin Williamson, claimed during
a radio interview. Patriotism and belief in your country are
good, but not to the extent of blinding you to what is really
happening in the twenty-first century.

In the forty years after the referendum of 1975, which
confirmed that Britain should be part of what was then the
European Economic Community, two significant things have
happened. One was that the newspapers, which had near
unanimously been in favour of us being members of the EU,
almost all turned against it, printing endless distortions and
untruths. The other was the founding of the United Kingdom
Independence Party (UKIP), while the Conservative Party,
as well as including a growing number of MPs who were
anti-Europe, had become overrun by members who were
blindly opposed to anything to do with Europe. The average
age of a member of the Conservative Party is fifty-seven.

This had consequences. For instance, in the Conservative
leadership election of 2001, the highly experienced and qual-
ified Ken Clarke, a pro-European, was beaten by Iain Duncan
Smith, who spouted a lot of anti-EU nonsense and whose
leadership didn't last two years before he was replaced by
the then pro-European Michael Howard, who subsequently supported the Leave Means Leave group during the 2016
referendum.

Most politicians understood that the UK received significant benefits from its membership of the EU, the world's largest trading bloc with 550 million citizens, but they hesitated

to show too much enthusiasm: and that wasn't only Tory politicians. When Tony Blair was Labour Prime Minister, it was said that he made strong speeches in favour of Europe – but only when he was over there. His speeches on home soil were always rather critical so as not to upset *The Sun* and the *Daily Mail*.

It was more problematic for the Tories, who feared that a growing number of their voters were drifting off to UKIP, which is why their leader, David Cameron, hit on the wizard wheeze of promising to hold a referendum on the UK's continued membership of the EU if he won the next election. Not that he thought he was risking much, as he didn't expect to get an outright majority.

But he did, and instead of doing the politician's usual thing of weaseling his way out of calling a referendum, he kept his promise, convinced that he was invincible and would win again. He even put himself at the head of the Remain campaign. Those decisions had consequences for this country which may be felt for a very long time.

CHAPTER 4

JOHNSON AND CHUMS

Leadership is essential for any successful campaign. Think of Winston Churchill uniting the country against the Nazis, or Genghis Khan founding the Mongol Empire, or Napoleon, until he got his army trapped in the Russian winter, or Lord Nelson, until he was shot on the deck of his ship HMS *Victory*. So we must look dispassionately at the leaders of the Leave and Remain armies.

Cameron led the Remain side in the belief that he could triumph under the slogan 'Dave could fix it'. He was overconfident about his own invincibility as so many Old Etonians seem to be and dismissive of UKIP's members, describing them as 'a bunch of ... fruitcakes', 'loonies' and 'closet racists'.

Like the Tories, Labour was officially on the Remain side – certainly most of their MPs and members were. Unfortunately Jeremy Corbyn was their leader at this critical time. Corbyn had spent his political career arguing against the UK's involvement with Europe, believing like others on the far left that it was a bosses' plot to keep workers down (unlike

the far right, who believed that the EU was a socialist plot).
He went through the motions of supporting the Remain
camp, but everyone could see his heart wasn't in it and he
was invisible for most of the campaign.

The rather smug, disjointed nature of the Remain campaign was in stark contrast to that of the Leave group. Various MPs and members of UKIP had spent years waiting for
this moment and they weren't going to fail to take advantage
of it. What gave them the greatest boost, however, was the
emergence of Boris Johnson at its head.

Johnson had never been particularly interested in the European issue, although he had worked for the *Daily Telegraph*
as its Brussels correspondent – writing nonsense stories
such as a proposal to ban bendy bananas – despite his father
having worked for the European Commission and being a
strong supporter of Britain's place in Europe. Johnson junior,
however, was mainly a strong supporter of his own career
prospects. Before the referendum, Boris Johnson actually
wrote two columns for the *Daily Telegraph*, one putting the
case for continued membership and the other the case for
leaving. At the last moment he chose to publish the Leave
one. He was old friends with David Cameron, who assumed
he would join the Remain camp, and his sister Rachel begged
him to back them. But at the last minute, Johnson announced
he was joining the Leave faction and became the figurehead
of their campaign.

The Leave campaign's secret weapon was Dominic Cummings. This single-minded fanatic had a sneering contempt

for everyone – MPs, civil servants, teachers (he revolution-
ised the education system when he worked with Michael
Gove while Gove was Education Secretary) and anyone who
knew anything. Although it was Gove who uttered the im-
mortally stupid sentence 'people in this country have had
enough of experts' during the referendum campaign, it more
than likely came from Cummings's fevered brain.

Dominic Cummings's rise and fall will be described later,
but for now it is enough to know that he was selected by
some wealthy Brexit backers to run Vote Leave, which was
the official campaign. There was another campaign, called
Leave.EU, which was led by the UKIP leader Nigel Farage,
who had made his name by denigrating all things European
except his German wife.

And so battle commenced, with one side blithely announc-
ing the dangers of leaving the EU and the other employing a
mixture of lies, distortions and xenophobia while painting a
picture of a Britain freed from the shackles of the European
Union which would be all positives and no negatives.

CHAPTER 5

THE COLD LIGHT OF DAY

It would be unfair to criticise voters for not understanding how the EU works. The truth is that hardly anyone did. Not politicians, not journalists, not even most academics, but following the result of the referendum, the cold light of reality began to creep in. What Leavers had dismissed as 'Project Fear' turned out to be worse than anyone had forecast, while the great new Britain that had been promised by Brexiteers was seen to be no more than an imaginary land of unicorns.

People in the twenty-first century know far more than previous generations, thanks not only to better and longer education but also to the huge amount of information on television, radio and the internet. Yet life today is also extremely complicated and very few us of know much about the way society, industry and other systems actually work.

Let's look at just one example. Hands up who had heard of the 'supply chain' until we left the EU? Hardly anyone – except the people who relied on it for their businesses. This is how it works. The motor industry, for instance, was quite basic before the EU's single market. Almost everything needed to manufacture a car, van or lorry was produced at the factory, from the body to the engine. Some components came from outside – electrical parts were probably made by a different company, but that was located down the road so the parts could be easily obtained. Tyres would have come from another plant, but that wasn't far away either.

That all changed dramatically, however, when the single market was launched in 1993. Now a car body could be made in England, parts of the engine in Germany or Spain or elsewhere in the EU, and other parts in other EU countries, and they could all be seamlessly brought together because there were no borders, no customs checks, no paperwork and no forms to fill in. But that ended when the UK decided to pull out of the single market (which it didn't need to, incidentally, and the Brexit leaders had all insisted during the campaign that it would never happen).

Suddenly there were mountains of forms that had to be filled in, miles of red tape to deal with and long lines of lorries queuing up at the Channel to get into and out of Britain. Leaving the EU made British goods harder to produce, which meant they were more expensive. The motor industry in particular had warned of the dangers of leaving, but they weren't believed. Anyway, hardly anyone understood what they were talking about; politicians and the media certainly didn't.

One of the defining moments of the referendum campaign came when Michael Gove, a passionate advocate of Brexit and at that time Lord Chancellor and Justice Secretary, was challenged about the warnings being given by industry leaders, which were in stark contrast to what was being claimed by the Leave campaign. He brushed aside their concerns with the aforementioned comment about experts. Presumably the next time he goes to hospital he will be happy to have any medical procedures performed by the catering staff rather than a surgeon.

There had also been warnings that many EU citizens who were working in Britain while we were members would pack up and go home. It wasn't going to happen, said the Brexiteers – and if it did, it would be no problem. Well, it did happen, and it caused appalling problems in hospitality, care homes and on farms.

There was a particular shortage of lorry drivers, because Continental drivers thought that it wasn't worth coming to Britain and going through the agonisingly slow procedure to get in and out of the country, so shortages of imported food and goods grew. The government said that this situation was happening everywhere, but that was exposed as a lie when pictures appeared online of supermarket shelves in France, Spain, Italy and other EU countries positively groaning with delicious fruit and vegetables, while in this country we faced empty shelves.

CHAPTER 6

COVID

New Year 2020 began with reports of a mystery virus in China. Within weeks a killer was sweeping the world. The virus has since claimed millions of victims and disrupted the lives of almost everyone across the globe. Education, health, business, leisure and travel, and the economy and governments of every nation were all affected by the Covid-19 pandemic.

An unknown respiratory infection with no known cure, the virus swiftly spread outside China. News footage of its impact on Italy, where it became rampant, was particularly shocking as it continued to surge across Europe. Hospitals and health services were buckling and medics battled a tsunami of death that was sweeping across the world at an alarming rate. Elderly people and the sick were particularly vulnerable, but coronavirus was killing the young, fit and healthy too, and Britain wasn't immune. By the end of January 2020, two cases had been confirmed here.

While some countries reacted quickly by imposing

lockdowns, travel bans and other restrictions, in the UK, life carried on as normal. Although frontline healthcare workers raised concerns regarding the country's ability to cope with a large-scale outbreak, Boris Johnson didn't appear bothered. In a televised press conference on 3 March, the Prime Minister reassured the country that the government would 'contain, delay, research [and] mitigate' the impact of the virus. His recipe for dealing with this deadly disease was to urge people to wash their hands regularly for 'the length of time it takes to sing Happy Birthday twice'. This did not provide a lot of protection from an airborne virus. Johnson also boasted that he had visited a hospital that day and had shaken hands with everyone he met.

There were no bans on big sporting events like the Cheltenham Festival and no travel restrictions, which meant that thousands of Spanish football fans were able to travel to England and watch Atlético Madrid play Liverpool in a Champions League match.

On 11 March the World Health Organization declared the coronavirus outbreak a global pandemic. In the UK, experts warned of a total collapse of critical care and urged social distancing restrictions. Johnson continued to pooh-pooh their fears although beds in intensive care units were already full. It wasn't until almost a fortnight later, on 23 March, that the Prime Minister finally acted and announced a national lockdown.

This was an unprecedented curtailment of freedom, more restrictive than anything during the Second World War, and was the biggest shutdown of society in our history. Only essential travel, for food shopping, exercise (of humans and animals), medical attention and travelling for necessary work, which included those working in healthcare, farming, journalism, policing and food distribution, was allowed.

Schools, offices, non-essential shops, pubs, restaurants, libraries, cinemas, sports centres, playgrounds and theatres were closed and places of worship were also shut. People weren't allowed to travel, go to school or work, visit family or friends or be beside elderly relatives in care homes, women in labour or the dying. Gatherings of more than two people in public were banned, which included social events like weddings and baptisms. Dentists and hairdressers were closed and social distancing was imposed, which meant long queues outside shops as only one or two customers were allowed in at a time.

Those walking or out for exercise weren't allowed to stop and chat or sit near each other on a bench. Those who could worked from home, while many also had to juggle that with home schooling. For many who were already lonely and vulnerable, lockdown meant total isolation. For those who lived in overcrowded conditions with no access to outside space, it was almost unbearable.

By 5 May, approximately 32,000 people had died from Covid in the UK – more than in Italy. Thousands more were hospitalised and critically ill, and those figures continued to rise. There were daily television briefings from the Prime Minister, other government ministers and public health experts like Professors Chris Whitty and Jonathan Van-Tam, who became household names.

Although local councils and communities, organisations like the BBC, charities, unions, businesses and individuals were quick and imaginative in responding to the crisis, with online learning, social events, food deliveries and other support mechanisms, all of our lives were completely upended by the decisions made by the government. They had been elected to run the country, but no one imagined it would be run like this. The impact of their decisions is still being felt across the whole of society and every aspect of our lives, from healthcare to housing, education and the economy to how and where we work, travel and engage with each other.

If anything demonstrates the importance of having good government, the Covid pandemic must be top of the list.

There were many questions that needed to be answered about this unrivalled crisis and there were demands for an official inquiry to investigate and hopefully deliver some of the answers. Yet the Johnson government prevaricated and delayed and it wasn't until June 2023 that public hearings of the Covid-19 Inquiry began. It will look into the government's response, the decisions taken during the pandemic, the impact they had, how well we were prepared for such a crisis and how we might do better in future. However, there are some things we do already know:

- There were no gowns, visors, swabs or body bags in the government's pandemic stockpile when Covid-19 reached the UK, despite the fact that, as far back as June 2019, the government was advised by its expert committee on pandemics to purchase gowns.

- There wasn't enough personal protective equipment (PPE) to keep health and care staff safe, so that ambulance crews and anyone working in a hospital or care home was risking their life every day they went to work. Many isolated themselves from their families to try to keep them safe.

- The chaotic testing before the vaccine was available meant that people, particularly the elderly, were discharged from hospital into care homes with Covid so that the virus spread like wildfire among extremely frail and vulnerable people: tens of thousands of them died.

- The 'furlough' scheme, which effectively meant that employers were given grants by the government so they could keep paying staff up to 80% of their wages during lockdown, cost around £70 billion. That is £70,000 million – about half the cost of running the NHS for a year.

- Scientists and pharmaceutical companies worked together to create a vaccine for Covid-19. On 2 December 2020, the Pfizer-BioNTech Covid-19 vaccine was approved for use in the UK, becoming the first to be authorised anywhere in the world.

- Billions of pounds of public money was spent on inadequate PPE. The Department of Health and Social Care lost three quarters of the £12 billion it spent on PPE in the first year of the pandemic due to inflated prices and kit that was not fit for purpose, including £4 billion worth of PPE that could not be used in the NHS and had to be disposed of at great expense.

- Some people, such as Michelle Mone, made a huge amount of money out of contracts for PPE, many of whom had connections to government ministers and the Conservative Party, but had absolutely no experience in this field .

- Between February and November 2020, 98.9 per cent of Covid-19-related contracts, valued at £17.8 billion, were awarded without any form of competition and, in most cases, without the necessary justification.

- Fourteen new companies founded in 2020, after the pandemic began, received contracts worth more than £620 million. Out of these, thirteen contracts to the value of £255 million went to ten firms that were less than sixty days old.

- The government's flagship test and trace scheme failed to achieve its objective of cutting infection levels, despite being handed £37 billion in taxpayers' cash, 20 per cent of the NHS's entire annual budget. The scheme had been assigned to the Conservative peer Dido Harding, a personal friend of Health Secretary Matt Hancock and former Prime Minister David Cameron, who, instead of asking the NHS and local councils to run the scheme, gave the work to two private firms.

- Poor ventilation in many public buildings meant they were unable to operate safely because they simply couldn't open windows and let air circulate. The pandemic and lockdowns laid bare bad housing and health inequalities, which would have a lasting effect on poorer people and ethnic minorities.

- Everyone learned how to make banana bread and Joe Wicks became a household name due to his online fitness videos. Lots of people discovered the joys of gardening and swimming outdoors, or they got a dog.

When that first lockdown was eased, social 'bubbles' were introduced, along with quarantine travel measures, so that people arriving in the UK had to self-isolate for fourteen days and tell the government where they would quarantine. These measures were enforced through random spot checks and £1,000 fines for breaking the rules in England. Face masks on public transport became compulsory apart from those who were exempt.

Then the Prime Minister got Covid. He became so ill that he had to be rushed to hospital, where he was placed in intensive care. At this critical moment for the UK, the country's leader was isolated and out of touch. When Johnson recovered and returned to Downing Street, a new controversy erupted. It was revealed that Dominic Cummings, Johnson's right-hand man who was sometimes referred to as the real Prime Minister, had travelled from London to Durham to stay in a cottage on his parents' farm, breaking the strict lockdown rules that he had played a major part in formulating and which everyone else was expected to observe. When asked why, while he was there, he had gone on a forty-mile drive into the country on his wife's birthday, he said it was so he could test his eyesight in case it had been impaired by the virus. The nation was incensed and incredulous.

But that scandal was nothing compared to 'Partygate', the series of gatherings and parties that took place in Downing Street during the lockdowns. These parties were attended by No. 10 staff and included the Prime Minister and his wife, special advisers, civil servants and other ministers. Among his denials, Johnson claimed that the parties were 'work related'.

In the summer of 2020, when the first lockdown ended with the hospitality industry in crisis after being closed for months, the government introduced an 'Eat Out to Help Out' scheme which provided diners with discounts in an attempt to boost the sector. It cost £849 million and was claimed by 78,116 outlets. Later analysis suggested that the scheme's greatest achievement was to help spread the virus. The subsequent spike in infections led the government to ban indoor and outdoor social gatherings of more than six people and the baffled British people struggled to keep up with what they were and weren't allowed to do.

In November 2020, a second lockdown was imposed because of surging infections, although Boris Johnson attempted to sweeten the pill by going on TV to pledge that he would not spoil people's Christmases by imposing a lockdown over the festive season. But then he did anyway. And by January we were into the third national lockdown.

These mixed messages caused confusion and distress. Court hearings were delayed, leaving the accused and victims of crime in limbo, businesses couldn't plan ahead, children lost out on education and social skills, and everyone lost out on time with their families, friends and colleagues. Not all could work from home and people with insecure jobs were facing poverty. Parents, dealing with home-schooling and bored children, suddenly recognised the dedication and value of teachers who were still running lessons online and, in some cases, teaching face to face.

Not only was the health service battling with the virus, people were still having accidents, and babies, and cancer and heart attacks. Waiting lists rose and people couldn't get to see a doctor. Social and mental-health care fell by the wayside and yet an already burnt-out workforce had to keep going.

On Thursday evenings, throughout the country people stood on their doorsteps to 'clap for carers'. It was a small token of appreciation for what they were doing. Yet, despite this genuine outpouring of recognition and gratitude for health and other key workers, many of them have since left their jobs, or resorted to industrial action to improve their pay and conditions, because clapping and rainbow posters don't pay the bills.

The pandemic brought out the best and worst in people – kindness, dedication and compassion alongside greed and selfishness. Those who could afford to skirted the rules and decamped to second homes. Supermarket shelves were often empty, some products were rationed and there were several instances of people trying to make a quick buck by selling the loo paper they had stockpiled. A video of an exhausted nurse in tears because she couldn't even find an egg for her supper at the end of a long, gruelling shift went viral. Builders, plumbers and electricians couldn't work because they couldn't get supplies and the cost of everything rocketed as these shortages were exploited for a fat profit. Yet, at the same time, all over the country, thousands of people did the shopping for their elderly and housebound neighbours, ran errands for them and made sure they were safe. It was a tale of two Britains.

Even tighter rules were introduced to curb the spread of the virus. The government announced mandatory hotel quarantine for people travelling to the UK from a list of high-risk countries. People were challenged or arrested by the police for walking outdoors, and massive fines were imposed on those foolish enough to organise large gatherings like raves.

By the early spring of 2021, the vaccine was being given to those most at risk of contracting the virus and a target was set for every eligible adult to be vaccinated by the summer. In England, face coverings became compulsory in most indoor venues such as cinemas, theatres and places of worship. People were once again advised to work from home.

Inconsistency, uncertainty and downright fear led to anger and frustration. There were anti-lockdown protests and conspiracy theories about the vaccine and Covid itself, yet the government insisted there could be no exceptions to the tight rules. This was symbolised by the moving sight of a frail Queen Elizabeth grieving alone for her husband, Prince Philip, in St George's Chapel, Windsor. That image of the monarch abiding by the rules resonated with thousands of families who had been unable to say goodbye to or comfort their loved ones. It also underlined the public fury at the Downing Street parties and the disregard for the rules by those who had set them.

- The UK had the highest number of deaths from Covid-19 in western Europe.
- On 20 January 2021, 1,820 deaths were recorded, the highest total in a single day in the UK.
- By 13 January 2023, the number of confirmed cases of Covid-19 in the UK was 24,243,393.
- Covid-19 led to an unprecedented increase in the overall number of deaths in England and Wales. It affected every group in the population and caused life expectancy in 2020 and 2021 to fall to the levels of the previous decade. The pandemic has exacerbated health inequalities which were already widening.
- Thousands of people are still suffering from the effects of 'Long Covid' and many thousands more have missed the early diagnosis and treatment of serious conditions, including cancer.

Covid changed us completely, not least because so much of what we do, whether it's work, study, booking a doctor's appointment or shopping has moved online. Our high streets and habits have changed beyond recognition. People couldn't have driving lessons or take driving tests and they couldn't use the library or go to church.

Children and young people lost years of their education and toddlers started nursery school not knowing how to interact with other children or adults after months of lockdown. Musicians, actors and entertainers couldn't find work and the production of films and television shows came to a halt.

The British Academy's independent report into the impact of Covid summed it up like this: 'The social, economic and cultural effects of the pandemic will cast a long shadow into the future .... with deep impacts on health and wellbeing, communities and cohesion, and skills, employment and the economy which will have profound effects upon the UK for many years to come. ... it exacerbated existing inequalities and differences and created new ones, as well as exposing critical societal needs and strengths. 'In sum, the pandemic has exacerbated existing inequalities and differences and created new ones, as well as exposing critical societal needs and strengths.'

They came up with a list of nine areas most affected by the pandemic:

- Increased importance of local communities
- Low and unstable levels of trust in governance
- Widening geographic inequalities
- Exacerbated structural inequalities
- Worsened health outcomes and growing health inequalities
- Greater awareness of the importance of mental health
- Pressure on revenue streams across the economy

- Rising unemployment and changing labour markets
- Renewed awareness of education and skills

Every single one of these requires strategic long-term thinking, new ways of working, engaging with people and funding. This means that our elected politicians have some serious work to do, to recognise what didn't work and why, support what did and look at a country emerging, forever changed by something that started on the other side of the world.

In June 2023, a survey of eight thousand people, conducted by Focaldata for the Institute for Public Policy Research, showed that the British public's trust in the political system has plummeted since the pandemic. The report found that just 6 per cent of the public had full trust in the current political system, while 89 per cent supported constitutional reform; only one in three trust Parliament to fulfil its core function of acting in the best interests of the UK electorate and subsequently an overwhelming majority supports reform.

This should worry everyone. It means that when it was tested, the government failed dismally and, once trust is lost, the ground becomes fertile for the rise of populists and dangerous conspiracy theorists.

Every single one of you reading this book will have been affected by Covid-19 in some way. How we reshape the future of the country depends on all of us using our voices and our votes to make sure we have political leaders who are up to the challenge.

COVID FRAUD

The Covid-19 pandemic was the greatest crisis to hit the UK since the Second World War, but it wasn't the only record-breaking phenomenon at that time. The country also witnessed what the Labour MP Dawn Butler described as 'the largest whole-scale fraud the country has ever seen'. Billions of pounds of taxpayers' money was siphoned off by fraudsters and channelled into the pockets of friends and associates of government ministers and other Tory MPs.

It is a scandal of enormous proportions which has led to limited investigation and virtually no criminal charges, and it seems inevitable that most of the wrongdoers will get away with their ill-gotten gains. Taxpayers have had to cover a bill for £1.7 billion of fraud across all lockdown schemes.

But that is of little significance compared with what happened in the PPE scandal. When Covid-19 first struck, it caused panic in the government, which overnight found itself having to find large quantities of personal protective equipment such as aprons and masks which were desperately needed to protect NHS workers as they struggled to treat patients suffering from this highly contagious disease. There were virtually no supplies being stored, so the government had to track some down and buy them urgently.

It is understandable that things had to be done in a rush during the pandemic, but how they were done is unforgivable. There were established companies who made the required equipment, or who could source it from suppliers around the world, but, on the whole, these companies were completely ignored. So where did ministers get PPE from? The answer is: from their mates, their political associates and people who had donated money to the Conservative Party.

These deals were done on a formal basis by setting up a 'High Priority Lane' – known as 'the VIP lane' – which allowed potential suppliers speedy and direct access to ministers, MPs and peers – but only Tories, of course. The sums of money involved were eye-watering. One thousand contracts worth £18 BILLION were handed out to companies which had no experience of PPE and some of which had only just been set up: yes, they were set up to take advantage of the Covid pandemic in which hundreds of thousands died, including many NHS workers, while a few greedy people saw it as an opportunity to make a fortune. The National Audit Office reported that almost £9 billion had been written off, including more than £4 billion on PPE that couldn't be used.

The contracts which attracted the most attention were those awarded to a firm called PPE Medpro, which had no experience of producing PPE but were handed contracts worth £80.5 million and £122 million. Half of that – more than £100 million – was pure profit. The company had been introduced to the government by Baroness Michelle Mone, a Tory peer who ran a lingerie company and had been ennobled after giving large sums to the Conservative Party. You might wonder what making bras and knickers has to do with PPE: not much presumably, as most of the Medpro supply could not be used.

The National Crime Agency launched an investigation into PPE Medpro, although Baroness Mone continued to deny she had done anything wrong.

Another lucky person whose connections seem to have allowed him to take advantage of the billions thrown at the pandemic problem is Alex Bourne. His good fortune was that he used to be the landlord of the then Health Secretary Matt Hancock's local pub. Bourne was awarded a contract for £40 million (from the taxpayer) for supplying millions of Covid-19 test tubes. While established companies couldn't get anywhere near providing supplies, Bourne managed it by simply sending Hancock a WhatsApp message. Easy when you know how, isn't it?

The contracts are only the tip of this iceberg. Hancock was found by the High Court to have acted unlawfully in failing to publish multi-billion-pound Covid-19 government contracts within the required thirty-day period. Mr Justice Chamberlain said that Hancock had breached 'the vital public function' of transparency over how 'vast quantities of taxpayers' money was spent'. The court ruled that the VIP lane was unlawful, though no one has been prosecuted for it.

The parliamentary Public Accounts Committee identified 'significant failings' in the management of PPE contracts that led to stockpiles of almost £4 billion worth of items not needed. It also concluded that suppliers were likely to have made excessive profits while providing substandard equipment.

The committee's chair, Dame Meg Hillier, said that 'the departure from normal approaches to due diligence, record keeping, decision making and accountability in relation to PPE contracts puts a stain on the UK's response to the pandemic.' The 'complete collapse' of long-established purchasing practice 'beggars belief' and she added: 'the taxpayer will be paying for these decisions for years to come.' This is worth remembering when the government insists that it doesn't have the money to give bigger pay rises to doctors and nurses.

COVID-19 INQUIRY

The inquiry has been set up 'to examine the UK's response to and impact of the COVID-19 pandemic and learn lessons for the future'. It is chaired by Baroness Heather Hallett, a retired judge and crossbench peer who has the power to compel the production of documents and call witnesses to give evidence under oath but doesn't have the power to bring criminal or civil charges against individuals or bodies and cannot force the government to adopt its recommendations.

- *The inquiry will hold public hearings which are expected to last until 2026.*
- *It has also encouraged people to share their experiences through the Every Story Matters section on its website.*
- *The inquiry is expected to last for years, with no date given for when it will end, and the cost is likely to run into tens if not hundreds of millions of pounds.*
- *The inquiry is split into several modules, interim reports will*

be produced at the end of each one and each hearing will last for six weeks.

- *Each module looks at different aspects of the Covid pandemic. Four modules have been opened so far, covering:*

1. *Resilience and preparedness*
2. *Core UK decision-making and political governance*
3. *The impact of the pandemic on the healthcare system*
4. *Vaccines and therapeutics*

Other issues to be covered include government procurement and PPE, test and trace, and health inequalities.

Other countries are conducting their own inquiries and some have already published their final reports.

The Covid-19 inquiry has already faced challenges in its attempts to gain access to WhatsApp messages and diary records held by Boris Johnson and the Cabinet Office, which the government argues it can only provide in redacted form. The government launched a judicial review objecting to Baroness Hallett's request for unredacted records, which meant that it was suing a judge whom it had appointed to keep certain messages out of the public arena. The government lost and was forced to provide the material as requested. The taxpayer footed the bill for this absurd challenge.

CHAPTER 7

UKRAINE, GAZA AND OTHER CONFLICTS

In 2022, nobody would have expected to see scenes reminiscent of the Second World War, with hundreds of thousands of people crammed onto buses and trains, in cars, and pouring out of railway stations clutching each other and a few belongings, escaping armed conflict and fleeing into an unknown future as war in Europe became terrifyingly real.

Nobody would have expected that a one-time comic and satirist who became President of Ukraine would become one of the world's most recognisable people, rallying his compatriots, his troops and urging the USA and Europe to help him fight Russia.

But the war in Ukraine had really started several years before, in 2014, when Russia took over, or annexed, Crimea. There was a lot of tut-tutting and condemnation of Russia's actions, but nobody did anything. So Russia, under President Vladimir Putin, just waited patiently, like a crocodile ready to pounce, and pounce he did, on 24 February 2022, when Russian forces invaded a largely unprepared Ukraine. Thousands of people have died in the conflict, including at least 10,000 civilians. Thousands more are missing, 3.7 million people have been displaced, and towns, cities and infrastructure across Ukraine has been destroyed. It's estimated that around 1.5 million homes have been destroyed, with direct damages to buildings and infrastructure estimated to have reached $135 billion.

Russia thought the conflict would be over quickly but didn't reckon on Ukraine's President Zelensky and the resolve of the Ukrainian people.

Millions of people around the world who knew little about Ukraine suddenly realised how important it was as a supplier of food and raw materials that are used in a wide range of manufacturing and construction. About a third of the world's wheat, a quarter of barley production and some 75 per cent of the sunflower oil supply – all critical commodities for keeping humans fed – come from Ukraine and Russia. The war's disruption to supply chains across the world had a huge and devastating impact on prices and the availability of products and materials.

The invasion has also increased the risk of a wider European conflict and strained relations between Europe, the USA and Russia. The war has compounded other global crises and will have wider impacts for international cooperation on issues such as arms control, cybersecurity, counterterrorism, global economic stability and energy security.

Russia's isolation has destabilised the global energy and resource markets but also means it is seeking stronger ties with states which are willing to partner with it, if not in direct opposition to the West, then certainly to have less cordial relations. China and India become more important to Russia, as does whoever is in the White House. The impact of the war in Ukraine cannot be underestimated, obviously in terms of human misery and loss, but also the financial cost and the country's relationship with NATO (the North Atlantic Treaty Organization), Europe and the USA, which has an impact on all of us, whether we like it or not. One very big question is how long Europe and the US will be willing to support Ukraine, whether financially or militarily.

GAZA

On 7 October 2023, the Palestinian terrorist group Hamas launched an unprecedented assault on Israel from the Gaza Strip, killing 1,200 people and taking about 240 hostages.

In response, Israel's warplanes carried out devastating air strikes across Gaza while its troops moved through the territory. Tens of thousands of Palestinians have been forced to flee, only to find the areas they were told to go to by Israel were then bombing targets. More than 25,000 Palestinians have been killed, including women, children, aid workers and journalists. Thousands more bodies lay beneath the rubble of buildings. More than 1,400 Israelis have been killed.

After the Hamas attacks, Israel shut its border crossings with Gaza, preventing supplies of food, water and medicine from entering the territory. Conditions for the people in

Gaza are dire and there have been widespread calls for urgent humanitarian support.Forty-one kilometres (25 miles) long and 10km (6 miles) wide, the Gaza Strip is located between Israel, Egypt and the Mediterranean Sea. Home to 2.2 million people, the narrow territory is one of the most densely populated areas in the world. Conflict between Israel and Palestine is not new but the war in Gaza is one of the deadliest, and the longer it continues the more fears grow that the conflict will spread, drawing in Lebanon, Syria, Egypt, Saudi Arabia, Russia and Iran.

In January 2024 the Secretary-General of the United Nations, António Guterres, described the Middle East as 'a tinderbox', saying, 'we must do all we can to prevent conflict from igniting across the region.' To some extent it already has. Towards the end of 2023, Houthi rebels, who control much of Yemen and are closely aligned to Iran, started attacking commercial shipping in the Red Sea, which they said was in support of Palestine. The USA and the UK launched air strikes on Houthi targets. The Red Sea is a vital shipping route but alternatives would add delays and costs to many goods, from food to furniture, being transported around the world.

There are scores of conflicts around the world. Some have been going on for years and many of them never make the news headlines, but there's no doubt that relationships between countries, the roles of international leaders and tensions thousands of miles away can, and will, have a profound effect on us in the UK.

CHAPTER 8

RULE BRITANNIA
– THE UK'S PLACE IN THE WORLD

'**R**ule Britannia', that little ditty which, depending on your point of view, swells the heart with patriotic pride and sees Britons reaching for the nearest Union flag (which was probably made abroad) to wave frantically, or is an uncomfortable, outdated celebration of the British Empire and its links to colonialism and slavery.

In 1740, when the words of 'Rule Britannia' were set to music, the British Empire was heavily involved in the slave trade and, along with Portugal, accounted for around 70 per cent of all Africans transported to the Americas. By the turn of the nineteenth century, the British Empire was the largest, richest and most powerful economic force in the world. That could not have happened without controlling the largest slave plantation economies. It is only relatively recently that people have begun to question Britain's view of its past – a view that celebrates power, wealth and influence but overlooks the means by which those were achieved, a view that's been taught to generations of schoolchildren.

The story of Britain that celebrates colonialism and imperialism is being challenged through protests and campaigns to remove or change the narrative around slave owners who had statues erected in their honour and buildings, schools and streets named after them. In 2020, protesters taking part in a Black Lives Matter protest in Bristol toppled a bronze statue of the seventeenth-century slave trader Edward Colston and threw it in the harbour. That act of protest triggered important conversations about Britain's past, what it is to 'be British' and put the question of reparations – compensation for the nations and peoples so damaged by slavery – back on the agenda.

The question of Britain's role in the slave trade is often dodged by those who instead prefer to celebrate Britain's role in abolishing slavery. While that doesn't address the more pressing issue, it is worth noting that the anti-slavery movement depended on expanded democratic participation in the debate, with British women and the working classes playing a crucial role by bombarding MPs with thousands of petitions urging them to pass the laws that eventually brought slavery to an end, and that took a lot more effort than signing an e-petition or 'liking' a social media post.

CHAPTER 9

THE SUN SETS ON THE EMPIRE

The British Empire gradually developed into the Commonwealth and by the middle of the twentieth century, the United States and the Soviet Union were the two global superpowers. Although Britain still wielded some economic and military might, it was no longer able to dictate world affairs on its terms. Japan, China and East Asia gained more global influence, as did the European Union, and Britain's status in the world shrank.

This country's claim to great power rests more upon what it was than what it is. There is something rather sad about the argument that because Britain was important in the past, it is still powerful today. It is like seeing a once-great sporting hero decline or a performer whose voice can't hit the right notes anymore or a once-grand hotel now threadbare and tired. Unlike sport or music, where memories of great games played or songs sung will always be treasured, Britain's backward-looking reliance on its past glories can sometimes appear arrogant and out of touch. To be a key global player, a country needs to demonstrate stability and competence, the ability to lead on the international stage and a clear understanding of the challenges that lie ahead.

So, where does Britain stand in the world today? Not where it used to, that's for sure. But that viewpoint is often criticised as being unpatriotic by those who refuse to accept that Britain might not be the powerful global player it once was.

Great powers are countries whose influence reaches across the world with consequences for everybody everywhere. With an empire that stretched across two-thirds of the world, Britain certainly held this position throughout the latter centuries of the last millennium due to its economic, military and cultural power. That dominance meant that Britain could often call the shots while the rest of the world followed.

Fast-forward through two World Wars, the Cold War, the Great Depression, the rapid growth of other world economies, global unrest and the enormous challenges of climate change, displaced people, pandemics, food insecurity, energy and water supplies, and Britain has been relegated to little more than a walk-on part on the world stage.

OK, maybe that's a bit harsh.

- Britain is a founding member of NATO, which was established after the Second World War to secure peace in Europe and resist the threat posed by the then Soviet Union.
- Britain is also a founding member of the UN (United Nations) and signatory to the 1948 Universal Declaration of

Human Rights, which formed the basis of the European Convention on Human Rights (ECHR). The United Kingdom was one of the countries that drafted the ECHR and was one of the first to ratify it in 1951.

- British diplomats are expected to abide by the Diplomatic Code and uphold its core values of integrity, honesty, objectivity and impartiality.
- Britain has some of the oldest schools and universities in the world and English is still the language regularly used at international conventions. The late Queen Elizabeth II was widely respected across the world and her contribution to diplomacy and foreign affairs over the course of her long reign was huge.
- Margaret Thatcher's relationship with US President Ronald Reagan strengthened the West's role in helping to bring about the end of communism.
- Tony Blair was, until the invasion of Iraq, the leader other world leaders wanted to talk to.
- Gordon Brown brought leaders of the G20 together to prevent the banks collapsing after the global financial meltdown.
- Boris Johnson's role in galvanising military support for Ukraine after Russia's invasion is worthy of respect.

So we do still have a place at the top tables and some influence, although the self-inflicted domestic political crises of the last few years, Brexit and Covid-19 have laid bare our self-delusion about our importance.

After Brexit, special trading arrangements were made for Northern Ireland as part of the wider withdrawal agreement signed with Brussels in late 2019. Yet Boris Johnson's government decided to 'reinterpret' that and brought in a new internal markets bill that even the former Northern Ireland Secretary, Brandon Lewis, admitted 'does break international law in a very specific and limited way.' This is probably not an argument that would work for a burglar in court.

Criticism came from across the political and international spectrum amid claims that Britain would be seen as a country willing to knowingly break an international agreement. It made our relationship with the US President, Joe Biden, particularly tricky, despite the so-called 'special relationship' between the two countries, and reduced Britain's diplomatic credibility.

That, along with the continuous anti-migrant rhetoric from the UK government, the shambolic failure to safely evacuate people from Afghanistan during and after the withdrawal of US and UK forces, and cutting our overseas aid budget by almost a quarter are just a few of the events that have severely damaged Britain's reputation for reliability and trustworthiness.

NOT ALL BAD

None of this is to take away the huge importance and influence of Britain's scientists, explorers, engineers and artists. The legacies of Shakespeare, Lennon and McCartney, Isambard Kingdom Brunel and Charles Darwin are respected around the world. Britain gave the world cricket, football, the BBC, Agatha Christie, Harry Potter and Stormzy. Indeed, it is often said that Britain's real influence comes from the 'soft power' base of arts and culture, which is presumably why the then recently elected Prime Minister Tony Blair was pictured grinning like a schoolboy with Noel Gallagher (the more cheery one from Oasis) at a Downing Street reception in 1997. Successive party leaders and Prime Ministers have tried, and usually failed, to jump on the cultural bandwagon in an attempt to look cool. Ironically, the arts, in all their forms, usually exist despite, rather than because of, government.

Britain's claims to be a great power on the international stage and an influential, vital and respected country seem questionable, if not downright deluded. It is fair to say that some of the country's decline is because of a shifting global power base in which China, India and Japan are jockeying for position. Although Russia is volatile, it is still of huge importance, and of course the United States, where Donald Trump's chaotic presidency wrought chaos.

Britain's place in the world, and what it can contribute to facing the massive challenges shared with the entire world, depends largely on recognising that times have changed and Britain must change too. If we want to be a global champion for democracy, human rights, law and order, then we need to rebuild a reputation for reliability and integrity.

That will only happen if we have conscientious and ethical people running the country and open and honest debate about what Britain, and being British, means.

- *On what was basically a triangular route from Europe to Africa, to the Americas and back to Europe, merchants exported goods to Africa in return for enslaved Africans, gold, ivory and spices. The ships then sailed across the Atlantic to the American colonies where African slaves were sold to work on sugar, tobacco, cotton and other plantations, and as domestics. The goods were then transported to Europe.*

- *It is estimated that Britain transported around 3.1 million Africans to the British colonies in the Caribbean, North and South America and other countries.*

- *Anti-slavery campaigners lobbied to end the trade for years and The Slave Trade Act, officially An Act for the Abolition of the Slave Trade, received royal assent in March 1807, but slavery wasn't properly abolished in the British Empire until the Slavery Abolition Act in 1833.*

- *The British government paid out £20 million in compensation to around 3,000 families who owned slaves for the loss of their 'property' when owning slaves was abolished in British colonies in 1833.*

- *This figure represented a staggering 40 per cent of the Treasury's annual spending budget, around £17 billion in today's terms. It was only paid off in full in 2015 by generations of British taxpayers.*

- *Enslaved people and their descendants received nothing by way of compensation.*

CHAPTER 10

A DISUNITED KINGDOM?

NORTHERN IRELAND

No consideration of the politics of Northern Ireland can ignore the stark reality that for thirty years a civil war was waged there with the loss of more than 3, 500 lives. Such was the sectarian hatred between Protestants, who were then a majority in Northern Ireland and passionately wanted to remain part of the United Kingdom, and Catholics, most of whom dreamed of being part of a united Ireland, that it seemed an impossible problem to solve. Something remarkable needed to happen, and it did when Tony Blair became Prime Minister.

Blair is increasingly derided for his time in Downing Street, but if he can be remembered for just one achievement, it should be bringing peace to Northern Ireland, although it is fair to say that his predecessor John Major laid a lot of the groundwork when he was Prime Minister.

The Good Friday Agreement of 1998 achieved a ceasefire between the warring factions and established an assembly and government to rule Northern Ireland in which both major parties would, and had to, serve. There then followed what had been unimaginable only weeks before. Sinn Féin, the leading Irish nationalist party which was widely regarded as the political wing of the IRA, formed a government with the leaders of the DUP, the ultra-Protestant Democratic Unionist Party. It was a historic feat, and although it did not end all the division, distrust, or even the violence, it has brought the people of Northern Ireland an almost normal life.

The agreement worked so well, and people who had spent decades violently opposing each other began to enjoy such extraordinarily good relationships, that it really did seem that Northern Ireland would finally be able to become a fully functioning country within the UK. The Good Friday Agreement laid down that only if a majority of the people in Northern Ireland voted in a referendum to choose to unite with the Republic of Ireland would it happen.

But no one could afford to be too optimistic about the future. The assembly and the government have been suspended four times for various reasons. At those points it seemed that there was still an uneasy truce in the province, and although Sinn Féin was responsible for some of the suspensions, the DUP became the hardliners.

They also played a key role in Westminster politics during Theresa May's premiership when she lost her overall majority after calling a snap general election in 2017. In order to muster a majority in Parliament, she asked the DUP's ten MPs to lend her their votes. They only agreed after driving a hard bargain which forced the Prime Minister to give Northern Ireland an extra £1.5 billion for spending.

The DUP lost the power to influence the British government when the 2019 election saw the Tories returned with a comfortable majority, but they retained their old power of simply digging in their heels and refusing to budge when the need arose: and they saw that when it came to Brexit.

Leaving the European Union has been a particularly difficult problem for Northern Ireland, as those who understood what it would lead to had forecast during the referendum campaign. A majority of people in Northern Ireland voted to Remain, as all political parties apart from the DUP had recommended, for a very good reason. Being part of the EU had been crucial to the success of the Good Friday Agreement and meant that the long, meandering border between the North and the South disappeared, thus allowing the easy flow of goods and people, so the countries' economies boomed.

During the referendum campaign, when Remainers asked what would happen to the border if the vote was to leave, Brexiteers brushed aside their concerns. They blithely insisted that nothing would happen and everything would remain the same: but it couldn't be.

With the United Kingdom out of the EU, there had to be a border somewhere, because the European Union needed to protect its rules, regulations and laws. That border could be where it had been, between the North and South of Ireland, *or* (and this is a very big *or*), it could be in the Irish Sea between the west coast of Britain and the island of Ireland.

When Theresa May was in charge of Brexit negotiations, she had said that no British Prime Minister could agree to a border in the Irish Sea. When Boris Johnson became Prime Minister, he insisted with his usual bravado that: 'there will be no border down the Irish Sea – over my dead body.' Anyone who has followed what happens when Boris Johnson makes solemn pledges will not be surprised to learn that a border *was* created in the Irish Sea. (Obviously, Johnson lived on.)

This decision created the biggest crisis with the DUP yet. The reason that they had been the only Northern Irish party to support Brexit was that they had wanted to distance Northern Ireland as much as possible from the Republic, whatever the economic consequences. Now they had a Brexit which both put Northern Ireland close to the Republic and distanced it from Britain. It was the worst possible outcome for them and they flatly refused to participate in the government unless it was changed.

When Rishi Sunak became Prime Minister, he attempted to come to a new agreement with the EU which would resolve this problem, although the obvious way to overcome it was to rejoin the single market, if not the EU itself. Proposals were thrashed out with Brussels' representatives in early 2023 and led to the Windsor Framework. This wasn't enough for the DUP, however, and there was a two-year standoff at Stormont during which there was no government in Belfast and which only came to a tortuous end in January 2024. Don't hold your breath.

As ever, the danger with Northern Ireland is that if there is no functioning government, the risk of violence is ever-present.

Yet there is another concern for the DUP: the party which won the most seats in the last local elections was Sinn Féin, an unthinkable outcome a generation ago. But this is a very different generation. Sinn Féin is no longer seen as connected with the IRA or violence and is now led by Michelle O'Neill, a very different face to the one the party had presented in the past and who became the first nationalist to become First Minister of Northern Ireland.

The people of Northern Ireland have made the clear decision that they want the province to be ruled by the ballot, not the bullet. But only the politicians can make sure that continues.

SCOTLAND

For 500 years Scotland had its own Parliament, as it was a separate country from England, but in 1707 it seemed a good idea, not to mention practical, to unite their Parliaments. And so Great Britain was born.

Centuries went by with little desire north of the border to restore independence, but in the latter years of the twentieth century that changed, partly because Scotland felt that England had purloined the spoils of North Sea oil and given little back. As the independence movement grew, Tony Blair decided that the way to placate Scottish nationalists was to promise that if he became Prime Minister, he would give Scotland its own Parliament again. Blair (who was born in Scotland) reasoned that if the Scots had their own power to make laws, the demand for independence would fade: how wrong he was.

The taste of having some control over their lives was like blood in the sea to a shark. Far from fading, the Scottish National Party (SNP) attracted much more support and swept to power in the new Scottish Parliament. Holyrood, the name for the Scottish Parliament, because it is next to the Palace of Holyrood (or Holyroodhouse, to give it its proper name), had been given an electoral system which Blair believed would ensure that no party could achieve a majority on its own, but the SNP was so successful that it was able to form a government without relying on any other party.

The SNP also had a remarkable leader in Nicola Sturgeon, who headed the party and was First Minister from 2014. A superb communicator, particularly when compared to the wooden performances of Theresa May and the bumbling Boris Johnson at Westminster, Sturgeon grew ever-more popular and showed great leadership during the Covid-19 crisis. Any of her government's faults were generally overlooked, not just because of her popularity and competence, but in contrast to the alternative 400 miles away in London.

This was a particular problem for the Labour Party. It has never been able to form a UK government without winning a majority of the seats in Scotland, and now its dominance of Westminster seats north of the border had evaporated. The forty-one seats it held in 2010 dropped to two. And with the decline in Liberal Democrat MPs after the collapse of the coalition government in 2015, the SNP then became the third biggest party at Westminster.

In the 2016 referendum on membership of the EU, while

there was a narrow 'No' vote in the UK overall, the people of Scotland voted by 62 per cent to 38 per cent to remain. And when the Tory government in Westminster dragged the country into the harshest possible Brexit, it became a great rallying cry for the SNP to give the pro-European Scots a special reason for splitting from England: an independent Scotland could become an independent nation within the EU.

The future looked bright for the nationalists, but as history shows, when you are walking under a clear sky, a dark cloud will suddenly appear on the horizon, and what a dark cloud this one was.

Quite unexpectedly, Nicola Sturgeon announced that she was standing down as SNP leader and Scotland's First Minister. Within hours, her husband, who was also the party's Chief Executive, also resigned and questions were subsequently raised about the party's finances, which cast a dark cloud over what had been the sunniest of political fortunes. Inevitably, it led to a slump in support and perhaps the end of the SNP's power and popularity, providing the Labour Party with some hope of reclaiming part of its power base in Scotland.

WALES

When Scotland was given its own Parliament in 1998, Wales was very much the poor relation. The Principality was only permitted to have an assembly, which meant that it had fewer powers and had to remain reliant on decisions taken at Westminster. But a decade later, the assembly was allowed to become a Parliament – Senedd Cymru, to give it its proper name.

For as long as anyone can remember, Labour was the overwhelmingly dominant party in Wales, with rock-solid support in the country's mining and steel communities. Yet as those industries faded and died, and the sense of community faded with them, Labour's grip on power loosened. It has continued to be the leading force in Welsh politics, although the Tories have maintained a toehold, unlike in Scotland, and the Welsh Nationalists have not managed to achieve the same breakthrough as their Scottish counterparts. So, although Labour has been able to form the government, it has had to rely on support from the nationalists.

The existence of a Labour government in Wales has handed a political weapon to the Tories. When they are accused of damaging the NHS in England, they retort: 'Ah, but look at Wales! Run by Labour and they have longer waiting lists!' It might seem like childish point-scoring (along the lines of 'my dad's got a better car than yours'), but it hits home.

Unlike Scotland and Northern Ireland, Wales did vote to leave the EU. Its farmers, largely dependent on sheep, soon realised that might not have been a good decision when cheap lamb from New Zealand began to pour into the country. The billions of euros in regional aid that had been pumped into Wales, which has some of the most deprived areas in the whole EU, was also under threat as the Westminster government dragged its feet over replacing it.

CHAPTER 11

IN IT TO WIN IT

A general election, which is when every MP has to stand down and face re-election unless they are retiring, must be held every five years. Every one of the 650 Westminster seats is up for grabs and the election result might mean a change of government. This does not mean, as we have seen in the past few years, that we get the same Prime Minister for the entire parliament or that a parliamentary term must last for five years. Elections can be called at any time and political parties can change leaders when they like. This is unlike most other countries. In America and France, for instance, a President can only serve two terms. In the UK there is no limit to the number of terms a Prime Minister can serve, assuming he or she still has the support of their party – something which cannot be assumed.

When MPs die or resign, a by-election is called outside the normal general election timetable. Local government elections occur at least every four years, not all councils going to the polls at the same time. Separate elections are held for the devolved Welsh and Scottish parliaments and Northern Ireland Assembly. Candidates who win seats in these elections do not become MPs in the UK Parliament at Westminster.

To exercise your right to vote you need to be on the electoral register for where you live, study or work. You can legitimately register to vote in more than one place (for instance if you have two homes in different authorities) but being registered at two addresses doesn't necessarily mean you get two votes except for local council elections in England, Police and Crime Commissioner and mayoral elections. When you are voting in UK Parliament elections, UK referendums, London Assembly and London mayoral elections you will need to choose one address and vote in only that area. Voting in more than one location is a criminal offence. When deciding where to register, you might want to think about where your vote could have the most impact, or the place you care about the most. If you're not sure you are registered to vote, check with your local council in plenty of time, not the day before an election. Anyone can apply for a postal vote, so if you might be away or you simply can't be bothered to go to the polling station in person, register for a postal vote: just remember to post it.

You might have noticed that the theme of this book is about the importance of voting, using the power each one of us has to decide who runs the country and how. Most importantly, there is no such thing as the right or wrong way to vote. It's your choice, it's secret and you can vote for whoever you like on the list, even if you tell your mates you voted the same way as they did. Voting is not boring, soppy or daft; it's your right and you should use it. Just imagine the different outcome if all the people who could have voted in the last election but didn't, had used their votes.

PUB QUIZ PRIME MINISTER FACTS

- *Robert Walpole is the Prime Minister with the longest single term of more than twenty years, from 3 April 1721 until 11 February 1742.*
- *Margaret Thatcher is the longest-serving Prime Minister in modern history, serving for more than eleven years.*
- *Liz Truss is the shortest-serving Prime Minister, resigning after seven weeks.*

THEY WORK FOR US?

The British parliamentary system grew out of a desire for the people to have more of a say in how the country was run, but there are many people who believe that most MPs, all political parties, and certainly the government, couldn't give a hoot about what the electorate thinks despite the promises they make when they want our votes.

In the run-up to the Brexit referendum, the Leave campaign's controversial claim that Brexit would bring £350 million a week to spend on the NHS was plastered on the side of a bus. Funnily enough, it turned out not to be true, but that's just one of many examples of promises not kept.

If you saw a headline that said, 'Government Incompetence and Money Wasting Reaches New Level', you probably wouldn't even bother to read the article, because we know that politicians are incompetent, make promises they don't keep and walk away from the consequences of bad decisions to enter lucrative consultancy jobs or the House of Lords. But that's not actually true either.

There are more than 60 million people living in the UK, all with different needs, ambitions and concerns. We all want a roof over our heads, to not be hungry or cold, and to be safe and cared for if we're sick or unable to look after ourselves. Yet, we are often quick to criticise when the government doesn't give us what *we* want.

Nobody enjoys paying tax but most of us recognise that public services have to be paid for that way even if individually we don't use all of them. What we can probably all agree on is our anger about wasting money, such as the £100 billion on the HS2 railway line before the plug was pulled on it, or the £32 billion cost of refurbishing the offices of the Education Secretary when hundreds of crumbling schools were denied funds.

The other thing that infuriates and frustrates people is the lack of joined-up thinking across government departments and the total absence of common sense. Spending cuts mean that local swimming pools and sports centres are closing while another government department commissions a report on why children need to be more physically active. There are schemes to encourage volunteering and community spirit while it has become harder for people to access village halls and community centres. We have campaigns to discourage car use at the same time as rural bus and rail services are being cut.

Since the 2000s, governments of various political persuasions have promised to fight childhood obesity. They have commissioned and published reports, but obesity is increasing, especially among children in deprived areas. Meanwhile, politicians dither and delay about introducing bans on multibuys and junk food advertising at the same time as they sell off school playing fields, get rid of school cooks, contract out school dinners and allow fizzy drinks and chocolate dispensing machines into schools.

Some people will argue that it is not for the government or the 'nanny state' to tell us what to eat or how much to drink, when to exercise, to use sunscreen when it's hot or to be careful on icy footpaths. Stating the obvious is a sure way to annoy people. Yet the other way to look at it is from a financial point of view, because it's our money. The billions of pounds that the NHS has to spend every year treating obesity-related diseases could be used for so many other things, like making sure that everybody can see a dentist. The smoking ban, introduced in 2007, has been hailed as a major benefit to public health, saving the NHS money, cutting smoking-related illnesses and saving lives, as well as reducing litter.

Billions of pounds of public money is wasted every year on reports, consultations and contradictory messages, and hiring very expensive management consultants. The gradual drip-drip of incompetence and inertia is enough to drive any sane person up the wall and it's another reason people have so little faith in politicians.

DON'T GET MAD, GET EVEN

One way to get even is to use your vote. Ask questions, ask more questions and then ask more questions. We need to challenge 'authority' more, to laugh at the nonsense, to expose the incompetence and stupidity, and above all, to behave like grown-ups.

If we have a government that treats us as though we are stupid and which becomes an overbearing but well-meaning nanny, people begin to rely on the state to make decisions for them, believing that 'they' know best. If we have a government that not only talks about but actually takes away personal rights and responsibilities, then people become unaware of what is being done in their name.

If we don't say 'no', then the government assumes we've said 'yes'.

We're all busy, hanging on to our jobs, paying the bills, juggling family commitments and trying to remember which day to put the recycling out to be collected. We're bombarded by anxiety-inducing news about our health, the food we eat, climate change, crime or international conflict. Sometimes it is just easier to keep your head down, mind your own business and hope for the best. But here's the thing: governments tend to do things that creep up on you, like clamping down on the right to protest or making it impossible to vote without photo ID.

If the only people who bother to vote are bigoted, racist, homophobic, puritanical warmongers while everyone else shrugs their shoulders and says, 'No point, they're all the same as each other', what's to stop laws banning women from working, making every school have lessons on Saturdays, curfews after dark and no free medical care for anyone who has ever smoked, had a drink, ridden a bike or is over sixty?

Over the past ten years or so, the government has shown its willingness to break international law, ignore human rights legislation and rush through measures without proper parliamentary scrutiny and debate. Good intentions like those to protect children and young people from abuse mean that anyone who has any contact with children must undergo a criminal record check. While it is illegal for registered sex offenders to change their name without informing the police, there is no legal requirement for victims or other organisations to be informed of any alteration, so that someone can reappear with a new name and no record and sidestep a law meant to protect the most vulnerable.

Politicians have immense power but they are just ordinary people, as flawed as the rest of us. We give them power if we vote for them, but we give them more power when we don't bother to vote at all because we do not challenge them. Not voting is the equivalent of turning a blind eye to crime because we 'don't want to get involved' and then moaning because criminals get away with their misdemeanours. We have more power than politicians because we can use our vote and make them work to win it from us, hold them to account with it and remind them that they answer to us, the voters, not the political party they belong to.

POWER TO THE PEOPLE

The whole point of Parliament is that MPs are elected by the people and given the authority to act on our behalf, so we expect them to consider new laws and other legislation that will affect our lives. We want them to argue about and discuss the detail in these regulations.

Parliament, which means the House of Commons and the House of Lords, spends a lot of time considering a bill before finally agreeing upon it and it becoming law. This process might seem complicated and time-consuming, and if a bill is controversial, like the Illegal Migration Bill, opponents will often be described as blocking legislation just to be awkward. Yet, as the process grinds on, there is an opportunity for pressure groups, campaigners and experts to express their opinions, even if their thoughts are ultimately ignored.

Britain's history is rich with protest and campaigns. Ordinary people, angry and impatient, have made their voices heard, forced governments to listen and got things done. The poll tax riots of 1990 put the boot into Margaret Thatcher; Bob Geldof challenged, and changed, attitudes to poverty and Third World debt; Joanna Lumley lobbied the government for the right of Gurkhas who retired before 1997 to settle in the UK, and won. The women who camped at Greenham Common, the Campaign for Nuclear Disarmament, the gay rights campaigner Peter Tatchell, the Countryside Alliance and the Sunday Trading lobby have all had an impact on politics and politicians by forcing issues into the public arena. Sometimes, campaigns have gone on to become more formally organised into groups and even political parties – the Greens, the Scottish National Party and UKIP for instance. Others became charities like Oxfam, the Samaritans and the Royal Society for the Prevention of Cruelty to Animals (RSPCA).

Without campaigns to change or introduce new laws, women wouldn't have the vote, homosexuality would still be illegal, animals and air quality wouldn't be protected, the NHS wouldn't exist and children would still be working in factories. You might even be relieved to know that MPs are banned from wearing armour or carrying weapons in Parliament, thanks to a law first introduced in 1313 and which still stands today. Gambling in a library is illegal, so is beating your rug in the street in London or walking a cow in the street in daylight.

ANYONE CAN JOIN

Pretty much anyone can stand for election to Parliament. As long as you are over eighteen, a UK citizen, and don't hold a politically restricted role – such as that of a police officer, civil servant or a judge – and you can pay the deposit, your name can go on the ballot paper and you can get on with campaigning.

But you will lose your deposit if you don't get at least 5

per cent of the vote, which, realistically, means convincing hundreds if not thousands of people to vote for you in a parliamentary election. That is why many people begin their political careers at the local level, for the town or parish council or in local charities or community groups. It is also easier to obtain the 5 per cent if you become involved with an established political party, where there will be opportunities to help with campaigns, meetings and events and you will have a chance of being selected as the official candidate in an election. Many people who become MPs begin their career working for their local MP.

POLITICAL ELITE

They may represent us, but do MPs reflect us?

- Just over a third of MPs elected in 2019 were women
- The average age of an MP is around fifty
- An estimated 10 per cent are from a minority ethnic background
- Almost 45 per cent of Tory MPs elected in the 2019 general election went to a fee-paying school
- 20 of Britain's 57 Prime Ministers were educated at Eton, including David Cameron and Boris Johnson
- 30 of them went to Oxford University and 14 went to Cambridge
- John Major, Prime Minister from 1990 to 1997, left school at sixteen and didn't attend university

- The UK has had three female Prime Ministers, all Tories, Margaret Thatcher, Theresa May and Liz Truss
- The Labour Party has never had a permanent female leader
- 7 per cent of MPs can be considered 'working class', in comparison to 34 per cent of UK working-age adults

There are MPs who have been lawyers, journalists, doctors and teachers. A handful have served in the armed services and there are a few farmers and business people, but Parliament is not truly representative. Previously, many Labour MPs came through the trades union movement, but the cost of campaigning and the time needed to do so mean that a political career is well out of the reach of anyone who doesn't have the time, the money or the backing of an organisation like a union.

It doesn't necessarily follow, then, that MPs who aren't like us are all out of touch with the real world, but it does mean that when people complain about a 'political elite', it does contain a grain of truth, particularly when you consider that many people in the media, business, the law and those running organisations and institutions come from similar backgrounds to the people sitting in Parliament. This lack of social diversity has been called the 'class ceiling' and it is another compelling reason to get involved in politics, even if only by using your vote. If you join a political party, you will have a say on who stands for election to local councils, as well as to Parliament. And who knows, it could be you!

CHAPTER 12

COUNTS VOTES ETC.

AND THEY'RE OFF...

For no particular reason, elections in the UK are usually held on a Thursday. The Prime Minister can call an election whenever he or she likes (unless the House of Commons passes a vote of no confidence in the government), but it must be no more than five years after the previous one. The monarch is then asked to dissolve Parliament, MPs become candidates if they're trying to retain their seat, there is frantic campaigning, leafleting and media activity, and the election typically takes place within twenty-five days of it being called.

A BOOTH AND STUBBY PENCIL

If you haven't chosen to have a postal or proxy vote, on election day you will need to go to your polling station, which is usually a school or a church hall. Polling stations are open from 7 a.m. until 10 p.m. and as long as you're in the queue to vote by 10 p.m. you will be allowed to vote.

At least, that is how it was until May 2023. Then, the government decreed that voters would need to have valid photo ID. Though what the government has decided is valid is a selective list. Critics of this blatant attempt to control those who are able to vote – and there are plenty of them – say this makes it harder for some people to exercise their fundamental democratic right. The election watchdog the Electoral Commission reported that around 14,000 would-be voters were turned away from polling stations during the local elections in 2023. The commission also raised concerns that voters with disabilities, people who are unemployed or those from particular ethnic groups could be disproportionately affected by the new policy. As the acceptable identification included forms like pensioners' bus passes but excluded bus passes for young people, the rules clearly tended to favour older people, who are more likely to vote Tory. In 2019 the Tory vote share among the over-65s was more than 60 per cent. (Note: It was a Conservative government that introduced the new ID rule. This is called 'gerrymandering', at least it was by Jacob Rees-Mogg, who was Leader of the House of Commons when the rule was pushed through Parliament.)

Inside the polling station you need to tell the staff your name and address so that they can check you're on the electoral register. You can vote before work, after work, on the way to the pub, while out walking the dog (there's even a hashtag #DogsAtPollingStations), and you don't need to dress up, although you will need to remove any face coverings so that staff can verify your identity in accordance with the requirements for voter ID.

Sometimes, volunteers for political parties will be hanging about outside the polling station and they might ask you for your poll number which is on your polling card. They are trying to work out how many people have voted and how many need encouragement.

Once you have received your ballot paper, which will tell you how many votes you need to cast, you go into a little screened area like a booth, and with the stubby pencil provided, you mark your ballot paper with an X – not a tick – next to the candidate you want to vote for. You must not write anything else on the ballot paper. Voting is anonymous and secret.

If you cannot fill in the ballot paper yourself, you can ask the polling station staff to do it for you, or you can ask someone you trust, such as a parent, carer or friend who is over eighteen and able to vote in the election to support you while you vote.

When you have filled in your ballot paper, fold it in half and put it into the ballot box. These are large boxes which will be clearly labelled, but if you are not sure just check with a member of staff. And that's it. You have exercised your democratic right, the right that people have fought and died for and are deprived of in so many places.

Then, the wait begins.

THE COUNT ... NOT DRACULA

Counting the votes begins as soon as the polls have closed and the black ballot boxes have been delivered to the sports hall or whatever building is being used for 'the count'. Counters, who are usually local government staff, empty each box onto a table, display the empty ballot boxes like trainee magicians and then compare the number of ballot papers that were in that box against the number recorded at the polling station or at the postal vote office. The ballot papers from different ballot boxes for each ward are mixed up to make sure that the votes remain secret. Then, the votes for each candidate are sorted.

Once all the votes have been counted and checked against the total number of ballot papers, the returning officer (usually the chief executive of the local council) shares the provisional result with the candidates and their agents. If the result is really close, they can demand a recount, but if they are satisfied that there's a clear decision, the returning officer will declare the result.

Before the results come in, there are hours and hours of speculation, analysis, graphics and gadgets as broadcasters and commentators swing into action. Reporters are sent to marginal seats where there might be a recount and especially to constituencies where a major upset could be a barometer of the final outcome, or a famous name could be toppled.

Sunderland in north-east England was the first constituency to declare its result for six general elections until they were beaten by Newcastle in 2017. It was claimed (by jealous rivals?) that Sunderland's traffic lights are rigged to hasten the delivery of the ballot boxes.

Most European countries hold their elections on Sundays, Denmark and the USA prefer Tuesdays, and Australia and New Zealand opt for Saturdays. Many countries don't start counting votes until the next day.

IF IT'S TUESDAY...

The Cabinet, which consists of Secretaries of State from all departments and a few other ministers, has been the committee at the centre of the British political system, and the decision-making body of the government, since the sixteenth century. It meets on Tuesdays, although between 1955 and 1963 Cabinet meetings were held on both Tuesdays and Thursdays. From 1945 to 1955, they were held on Mondays and Thursdays, and before the Second World War, they were usually held on Wednesdays. When Gordon Brown became Prime Minister in June 2007 he moved the meetings from Thursdays to Tuesday. These changes play havoc with the diary, but at least the Cabinet has been meeting in the same room in Downing Street since 1856.

THE DECIDEDLY DODGY HISTORY OF DOWNING STREET

Downing Street stands on the site of a medieval brewery, but whether that's where the phrase 'couldn't organise an event in a brewery' comes from, nobody knows. Sir George Downing was a traitor, a spy and certainly a dodgy property developer who realised that building houses on prime London land was a way to make money quickly. It took him thirty years to get hold of the land where Downing Street is now, and once he got the lease, he pulled down the existing properties and built a cul-de-sac of fifteen or twenty terraced houses. Like most dodgy property developers, Downing's houses were cheaply built, with poor foundations for the boggy ground. He even had mortar lines drawn on the houses to look like neat, evenly spaced brickwork. Samuel Pepys, the great diarist, called him a 'perfidious rogue'.

The current No. 10 started life as No. 5 and was not renumbered until 1787. It was originally made up of three houses joined together: the cheap terrace at the front, a modest cottage next door and a much grander building at the back which overlooks Horse Guards Parade. The house at the back belonged to the Countess of Lichfield, daughter of Charles II, and quite possibly the first aristocratic NIMBY. She was furious at the new houses being built so close to her and complained to her father, who suggested she got 'Mr Surveyor to build up your wall as high as you please.'

'Mr Surveyor' was Sir Christopher Wren, who, most famously, had designed and built St Paul's Cathedral, along with other buildings including the Royal Hospital Chelsea and the Old Royal Naval College. Probably the combination of Wren, the King and his extremely annoyed daughter meant there wasn't much point in complaining about the lack of planning permission.

The last private resident of what was to become the most famous address in the country was a Mr Chicken, who moved out in the early 1730s ... presumably to cross the road. Around the same time, the posh house at the back, the terraced house at the front and the cottage were knocked together. In 1735, the First Lord of the Treasury and Prime Minister Sir Robert Walpole moved in but refused to accept the Downing Street house as a gift from King George II. Instead, Walpole said it should be the home of future First Lords of the Treasury, and to this day, that is engraved on the brass letter box. By 1839 the area was seedy, with brothels and gin palaces, and there were plans to demolish Downing Street.

Benjamin Disraeli, who is famous for many things, but not especially plumbing, moved in to No. 10 in 1877 and splashed out £150 3s 6d on a bath with hot and cold water. Three years later William Gladstone coughed up an astonishing £1,555.5s on furniture, had electricity and telephones installed and probably would have gone for a bit of decking and a pizza oven out the back had it been fashionable then.

No. 10 is grand, has lots of rooms for posh dinners and receptions and a nice garden, which we now know was ideal for the 'bring your own booze' parties held while the rest of the country was in lockdown. It contains a maze of offices and meeting rooms, off-street parking and is handy for the office, but you can't choose your next-door neighbour, as No. 11 is the official home of the Chancellor.

Anyone over fifty probably remembers that you used to be able to walk up Downing Street and have your photo taken beside a long-suffering policeman on the doorstep. But in 1989, fears of a terrorist attack meant black steel gates were installed at the end of the road. Two years later, the IRA launched a rocket attack on No. 10 while the Prime Minister, John Major, and the Cabinet were meeting. No one was hurt, but the result was the fortification of Downing Street as it is today.

CONSTITUENCY FACTS

- *There are 650 MPs, each representing a constituency.*
- *A constituency has no physical size restrictions; it is all about the number of people who live there, which is around 70,000.*
- *London, Birmingham, Manchester, Bristol and other urban areas have several constituencies and several MPs, not always from the same political party.*
- *Even if MPs are from different political parties, they will often work together on big issues that affect their constituents, such as major planning developments, changes to health or transport facilities or changes to employment like the closure of a big local employer.*
- *Even if you didn't vote for them, your MP's job is to represent you.*
- *MPs have a constituency office and hold regular surgeries where you can make an appointment to have a private meeting.*

- *In theory, anyone can turn up at the House of Commons and ask to see their MP, but the tight security and MPs' busy diaries mean it's probably easier to write, email or phone to make an appointment.*

- *Your MP won't be able to help you in private disputes with neighbours, an employer, with family matters or with companies that have sold you faulty goods. They can't get involved with decisions made by the courts. People often take a problem to their MP because they don't know who else to turn to.*

- *MPs may have a local councillor at their constituency surgeries to help people whose problems are connected to services like social care, housing or education that are provided by local authorities.*

- *You might never need to see or speak to your MP, you might not even know what he or she looks like, but you can bet that once there's an election they will be all over you like a rash, because the only way they can remain your MP is by getting enough votes to keep them there.*

CHAPTER 13

MONEY, MONEY, MONEY

'It's the economy, stupid'. That slogan was the key message of Bill Clinton's successful campaign to become the US President in 1992. It is ironic, then, that for many people, when politicians, journalists and commentators start talking about the economy, many of us feel, well, stupid.

The economy broadly describes the state of the country's finances. This includes what we export, what we import, what we owe and what we can spend. The state of the economy has a massive impact on all of us in terms of jobs, public services, what we earn and how much things cost.

The production, exchange and consumption of goods are the basics of an economy. We trade goods, products and services locally, nationally and internationally. The more productive we are, the better the economy, which, in theory at least, means a better standard of living for everyone, as well as investment in public services and infrastructure, including roads, hospitals, schools and railways.

Governments try to shape the country's economy through

spending and taxation. Yet, because the world is so inter-connected through trade, labour and natural resources like water, oil, gas and precious metals, individual nations cannot always mould the economy in the way they'd like to. As we have seen with the war in Ukraine, what happens thousands of miles away can have a direct impact on what we can buy and how much it costs.

The Treasury is the government's economic and finance ministry which controls public spending and works to ensure the country's economic growth. The Chancellor has overall responsibility for the Treasury and relations between Prime Ministers and Chancellors are traditionally fraught, a situation that is made even trickier since they live next door to each other in Nos 10 and 11 Downing Street. Prime Ministers like to promise money for things the public want, while Chancellors say that, no, the country can't afford it.

The Budget, which is usually an annual event, is when the Chancellor reveals the state of the UK's finances, how much money will be allocated to public spending and how much goods, people and services will be taxed.

We all pay tax, whether it comes directly out of our pay packets or indirectly, through the tax we pay on petrol, alcohol, flights, clothes and kitchen fittings, as well as the bill for the actual fitting.

GDP is the acronym for gross domestic product, which is the total value of the goods and services produced in a country during a particular period.

The rent or mortgage you pay is influenced by the

economy, as is the amount of money you need to cover basic living expenses. This is where inflation comes in. Inflation means the rate at which prices increase over a certain period of time. It is usually one of the most important measurements because inflation is about the cost of living and is quite often outside our control. The war in Ukraine and terrible floods and droughts across the world have had a huge effect on the cost of everything from fuel to tomatoes. Those costs are then passed on through the supply chain to consumers, which then has an impact on what we need to earn to buy food, pay rent, run a car, use public transport or go on holiday.

The stock market is where investors buy or sell shares in companies and it can react very dramatically to global or national events. Liz Truss, who was Prime Minister for just a few weeks in 2022, managed to cost the country £30 billion after markets reacted to her disastrous mini-budget. This left a huge hole in government finances which, in turn, meant either higher taxes or cuts to public spending, or both as it turned out.

The rate of employment is important because a growing economy generally means more job opportunities, which means more people paying tax. Similarly, the more profit a business makes means that they should also pay more tax.

It is then down to the government to decide how it wants to spend the tax. It can be invested in education, housing and health or on projects like HS2, or even given back in tax cuts.

When you decide who you want to vote for, locally or nationally, it is important to look at what their party say it is going to do with your money. Traditionally, the Conservative

Party tends to believe that people should pay less tax and be able to decide for themselves what they do with their money, while Labour and the Liberal Democrats have a stronger commitment to investing in public services which traditionally means higher taxes, although the current tax-to-GDP ratio after all these years of Tory rule is the highest it has ever been.

Some extremely rich people use complex ways and clever accountants to minimise the tax they pay, although they might be happy to support projects or charities close to their heart. This is a pretty rough idea of philanthropy, which is to help other people, usually by making generous donations to good causes. This is positive up to a point, because some people argue that philanthropy is a way of atoning for past 'sins' – for example, families that have made their fortune through slavery or in the pharmaceutical industry have been very generous benefactors to the arts. Other donors simply want something named after them so it's a vanity project but, equally, there are people like Dolly Parton, Bill Gates and Elton John who have given millions to support long-term projects that have really made a difference to people's lives.

Ordinary people can also be incredibly generous. In the UK in 2022, the public gave £12.7 billion to charity and they support food banks and charity shops with donations. Yet many organisations can't function without the security of funding, whether that's actual money or rent-free space, and a lot of charities and volunteers are plugging the gaps that councils and other institutions can no longer afford to.

There are a zillion ways to judge how successful an economy is, but perhaps the easiest, most humane way is to look at the gap between the rich and poor, to look not only at the value of stocks and shares but at whether inequality is getting better or worse.

The UK has a very high level of income inequality compared to other developed countries. The official figures for 2022 show that incomes for the poorest 14 million people fell by 7.5 per cent, while incomes for the richest fifth of the population went up by 7.8 per cent.

CHAPTER 14

TAX AND BENEFITS

Britain will spend £135 billion on old-age pensions by 2025, which is considerably more than on education, policing and defence combined, according to official figures. The cost of pensions has been rising sharply because of the 'triple lock', which means that they increase by whichever is higher of the annual increase in average earnings, inflation or 2.5 per cent. That is great if you're a pensioner, but not so good for the younger people who are going to have to pay for it.

There are now more people aged sixty-five and over in England and Wales than children aged under fifteen, an increase of 20 per cent over the past decade, which means fewer young people will be working to pay for the pensions and cost of social care for older people.

When we talk about 'the welfare state', we usually mean benefit payments that include pensions, unemployment, child benefits, income and disability support. The idea behind these is that they protect families from hardship, reduce inequality and support disabled people. The benefits system provides practical help and financial support if you are unemployed and looking for work, and provides additional income when your earnings are low, if you have children, are retired, care for someone, are ill or have a disability.

The modern UK welfare state was founded in 1948 with the aim of providing 'cradle-to-grave' protection, including welfare payments to help people through temporary difficult periods, such as sickness and unemployment. But there is no definition of what this 'safety net' is meant to cover and the amount is decided by the government.

Around £100 billion is spent each year on working-age benefits, predominantly for those on low incomes or with disabilities. Politicians of all parties have to grapple with the cost of benefits, the resentment of people in work paying for those who aren't, and the notion of the 'undeserving poor', which is frequently cited by some sections of the media when they portray a family on benefits lounging about in front of enormous TVs, smoking, drinking and living off takeaways. (In 2014, Channel 4 broadcast a series called *Benefits Street* which sparked a huge media and political controversy about 'scroungers'.)

Politicians and policymakers have to decide whether, and how, to target benefits at those in low-wage jobs, those who can't work, families, or people with disabilities. One familiar criticism of benefits is that they discourage people from working, while complex and unwieldy systems make it really hard for people to claim benefits at all. There is also the stigma of even applying for benefits, which extends to receiving free school meals or simply asking for help.

Years of austerity and cuts to funding have pushed many people into poverty, including those who have jobs. The government has cut the value of working-age benefits in seven out of the last ten years.

In the summer of 2023 all the medical royal colleges, a range of charities, healthcare and children's organisations called on the government to guarantee that universal credit would cover basic survival. These organisations cited what poverty means: 'people unable to afford enough food because their incomes are simply too low ... people who are forced to miss hospital appointments because they can't afford the bus fare ... people missing or reducing their medication because they can't afford the prescription, or people with diabetes who risk serious complications from going without food.'

The Joseph Rowntree Foundation calculated that £120 a week was the bare minimum for one adult: £37 for food, £35 for energy, £6 for clothes and shoes, £8 for communications (phone/internet), £16 for travel and £13 for everything else, including toiletries, bank charges and cleaning materials. This amount would still constitute hardship, but not utter destitution, which the foundation defines as an income below £95 a week.

Benefits are funded by taxpayers. We all pay tax even if we are not working, on fuel, on goods and services and on savings. If we are working, we will also pay National Insurance contributions, which go to the government. If the amount we are allowed to keep – our personal allowance – before paying tax doesn't increase, then even a small increase in hourly pay could tip many people into paying tax and actually being worse off.

Benefits do not just mean income or payments; they include free prescriptions, free or reduced travel, disabled parking permits, help with specialised equipment for people with disabilities and access to other services, such as support for new parents, especially those from more deprived areas.

Hundreds of thousands of people currently enjoying a comfortable retirement will have also had the luxury of free university education, many will also have private pensions from their previous jobs and have been able to buy or rent somewhere to live much more easily than young people today. Equally, there are thousands of pensioners without those comforts who live in poverty and suffer from loneliness while having to face the very real worry of how to pay for social care when they can't manage by themselves.

The cost of social care is enormous and growing. People are living longer, often with a number of complex medical conditions. Successive governments have promised to deal with the problem but have failed lamentably. People who are well enough to leave hospital can't do so because there is no at-home care package in place, which means there is huge pressure to free up hospital beds for other patients. There is also a shortage of people working in social care. The government has cut funding in this area, although it promised to recruit and train more carers. Often, older people have to sell their homes to afford to enter a residential home that is miles away from their family and friends and of dubious quality.

Because there is a certain section of society that thinks people should 'learn to stand on their own two feet', 'shouldn't have children if they can't afford them' and 'should learn to go without', politicians don't want to be seen as 'soft on scroungers'. Yet life is never this straightforward. People lose their jobs, become ill, are abandoned by their partners, are bereaved, have to care for relatives or experience any of the number of other things that can and do happen to change someone's life. That is when they need help, support and dignity, not penny-pinching cuts and sneering from those who haven't yet fallen on hard times.

Imaginative and thoughtful politicians might view benefits, another way and instead of thinking about 'handouts' could consider how to improve the balance. They could raise the level of earnings above which National Insurance contributions (NICs) are paid and which would benefit people on lower wages. They could offer support for children through child benefit or tax credits, alongside schemes like the very successful Sure Start introduced by Gordon Brown, which was a programme to support young children and their families, particularly in disadvantaged areas. They could focus on preventive healthcare to help keep people fit and healthy and less likely to have to give up work and rely on benefits. They could stop the tax-avoidance schemes used by wealthy people and companies who pay a tiny fraction of tax on enormous profits, companies like Amazon, whose main UK division paid no corporation tax but instead received a tax credit of £7.7 million in 2022.

- *The youngest people in England and Wales are in suburbs and commuter-belt towns outside major cities.*
- *Barking and Dagenham has the largest proportion of young people: 24.5 per cent of the population is under fifteen years old. Slough in Berkshire (23.5 per cent) and Luton in Bedfordshire (21.9 per cent) follow.*
- *28.5 per cent of Birmingham's population is made up of those aged 0–19. This compares with 23.1 per cent across England and Wales.*
- *Nearly one in five people are aged over sixty-five.*
- *The richest 1 per cent of households own assets worth at least £3.6 million, while the poorest 10 per cent own less than £15,400.*
- *The top 10 per cent of households own 43 per cent of all the wealth in Great Britain.*
- *Between April 2022 and March 2023, the Trussell Trust distributed nearly 3 million emergency food parcels – an increase of 37 per cent on the previous year – and more than 1 million of these parcels were distributed for children.*
- *An adult reliant solely on benefits is expected to live on £85 a week, £67 for under-25s.*

CHAPTER 15

EDUCATION

It is difficult to believe how much education has changed in the past fifty years. Back then, only about 15 per cent of children – the so-called 'clever' ones – were educated as if they would ever amount to anything and not even 5 per cent continued their schooling beyond the age of sixteen (and it had been fourteen until 1918). The range of subjects available to study was restricted to not much more than English, maths, French, history, geography and religious studies.

Of course, even that was a huge improvement on what came before – which was no schooling, except for the sons of the rich (sorry, girls), until the middle of the nineteenth century. It wasn't until well after the Second World War, when comprehensive schools were introduced and the divisive eleven-plus exam was abolished almost everywhere, that schooling blossomed. At last, it was hoped, every child would have the chance of a good start in life. Naturally, there were still many problems, but it was a big improvement, even if some Neanderthal politicians continued to want to drag the country – and children – back to the days of dumping youngsters who couldn't surmount the eleven-plus hurdle on the educational scrapheap.

Schools continued to be funded by local councils whose education committees maintained control over them. That has changed dramatically this century, as both Labour and Tory governments decided that schools should be taken out of the control of local authorities and be run by other bodies. They decided that these shouldn't be called 'schools' anymore, but gave them the grand name 'academy', a word that seems like a throwback to the Victorian era. Standards did improve for most of these schools, but at a price. Their organisation often looked more like a commercial body, with a 'chief executive' – usually not much more than a glorified head teacher – who often earned a fortune, which meant that part of their job description was to keep teachers' pay down so that they could balance the books. This partly explains why teachers have recently taken the rare decision, for them, of going on strike.

The 'academisation' of education included the introduction of the idea of 'failing schools' to describe those where pupils didn't achieve as highly as in other schools. This designation could be useful in improving standards but sometimes led to an unfair comparison: it can hardly be right to compare a school in a deprived area with many one-parent families and high unemployment with another in a middle-class area in which affluent parents can afford to hire personal tutors and provide their children with computers and an array of books. This stark difference became particularly noticeable during the Covid-19 lockdowns, when schools were closed and children were expected to be 'self-educated' at home. That was fine for those who had a room in which to work and their own laptop and internet access, but meant children in cramped conditions who couldn't access their schoolwork online were at a terrible disadvantage.

These were also the youngsters whose lives had already been made harder by the significant changes made to the education system by the Education Secretary, Michael Gove, after the 2010 general election. He was obsessed with the belief that every child could be educated to the same standard and that they could all be forced to study and learn as if they had the same brain power as Albert Einstein. This is like insisting every pupil should be able to run 100 metres as fast as Usain Bolt. In this fanatical campaign, Gove was driven on by his sidekick Dominic Cummings, who played such a leading role in the Brexit referendum. Their policy aimed to create an education system that was great for brainboxes like them but, in the process, made learning inaccessible to many young people. For instance, they didn't want children to read anything except 'classics' – no matter how difficult they found reading – and forced complicated maths on young people, even if they struggled with simple sums, in the belief that all these children would be able to become brilliant engineers. Except, of course, most of us can't.

More and more exams were introduced. This country has the most examined children in the world. Formal tests used to start not long after little ones began at primary school, with SATs at seven and eleven, but that wasn't good enough for the government. Since 2021, four-year-olds have been given formal tests when they start in the reception class, while some countries with a more successful education system don't even let children start school until they are seven.

Although the dreaded eleven-plus, which singled out a small proportion of children as good enough for grammar school and rejected the rest as too stupid to bother with, was abolished when comprehensive schools were introduced, there is actually far more testing now. We no longer send children up chimneys or force them to work in sweatshops, but we torture them with exams instead. That is fine if you can cope with exams, but it is awful for the many young people who struggle with them. These children may be brilliant at all sorts of other things, but the education system brands them as failures for life. Some manage to rise above that and make successful careers for themselves but that doesn't excuse the way that children are treated at school.

Until the 1960s, university was reserved for only a small proportion of young people. This amount increased in the second half of the twentieth century and Tony Blair's Labour government set a target of getting 50 per cent of school leavers to attend university. This was never quite achieved, but it isn't far off.

Apart from the big increase in the number of students entering higher education, there is another major difference between university education now and fifty years ago: it used to be free. In fact, not only did students not have to pay tuition fees, they were given a grant. Tuition fees of £1,000 a year were first introduced by Labour in 1998, rising to £3,225, but the coalition government kept increasing them until they reached £9,250, meaning students had to take out ever-larger loans. The Tories also sold the debts off to a private company, which increased the interest rate and insisted young people began to pay back their loans as soon as they left university and were earning £22,000 a year.

At least the £9,250 fee has not been increased for several years, but that has left universities struggling to raise enough money as inflation has soared, so many are trying to attract more foreign students who are charged much higher tuition fees.

The student loans system has a long-term impact on those who attend university. It has been calculated that they will pay the equivalent of a 9 per cent 'graduate tax' on their earnings for forty years, which the money saving expert, Martin Lewis, has called 'a lifelong graduate tax for most'. Yet how much did the politicians who inflicted that on today's young people have to pay when they went to university? That's right – nothing.

CHAPTER 16

HEALTH

Among the many sayings attributed to Winston Churchill is: 'healthy citizens are the greatest asset any country can have.' A healthy society is likely to be more productive and economically successful for the simple reason that healthy people are able to work, earn, spend more money, pay more taxes and not use health and welfare resources. Good health is not just determined by the genes we inherit but by many other factors, including where we live, the air we breathe, the work we do, the food we eat, access to fresh air and exercise, social networks and activities and health and welfare resources.

The National Health Service, founded in 1948, has long been the envy of many other countries and is revered by the public, but it is creaking at the seams, there are huge staff shortages, lengthy waiting lists, crumbling hospitals and dysfunctional systems. Nearly all politicians promise to keep the NHS intact to continue providing free healthcare for everyone, but the realisation is dawning that we need to have a grown-up conversation about what we expect from a national healthcare system, how it should be funded and how it can be made more efficient.

The NHS spends just 5 per cent of its massive budget (£190 billion in 2022) on preventive healthcare, yet many of the conditions that make people ill are preventable. It is estimated that within the next ten years, Type 2 diabetes alone, one condition of diet-related disease, could cost the NHS 1.5 times what treating all cancers currently does. Obesity, inactivity, chronic respiratory conditions, alcohol and drug abuse and Type 2 diabetes can be, if not avoided completely, then managed. Public health bodies need to work alongside housing, transport, environment and education if we are to have a county where people are as fit and healthy as possible and those that need it can easily access treatment, medical interventions and support.

Poor-quality housing, which is prone to damp and mould and expensive to heat, can cause asthma and other respiratory diseases, as does air pollution from traffic. Obesity causes heart disease, Type 2 diabetes and hypertension or high blood pressure. Lack of exercise, a poor diet rich in processed food containing high amounts of fat, sugar and salt also contributes to poor health, while social isolation has a massive impact on mental health. All these conditions are avoidable and preventable.

COVID AND INEQUALITY

The Covid pandemic exposed many health inequalities in the UK. Infection and mortality were much higher among

HEALTH

older people, people from certain ethnic backgrounds and the disabled, with the risk of death during the first wave three times higher for disabled people and Black African men in comparison to non-disabled people and white men. This was partly due to existing health conditions, but that in itself begs the question of why some groups were more prone to such conditions?

More than half of the UK population has had Covid-19 since the beginning of the pandemic and millions of people have developed Long Covid, suffering debilitating long-term effects and being unable to work, study or lead anything like a normal life. More than 200,000 people in the UK lost their lives to Covid-19, and other factors, such as delayed cancer diagnoses owing to being unable to access hospital appointments, have resulted in additional deaths. We may never know the true impact of the pandemic on our long-term physical and mental health, or on the NHS, but we do know that questions about health prevention and healthcare and inequality in the UK existed before the pandemic and that their impact goes way beyond it.

So much regarding your health depends on where you live because there's nothing uniform about healthcare provision. Some GP surgeries have a whole load of other specialist clinics and services, but others don't and it's easier to get a ticket for a Taylor Swift concert than an appointment to see a doctor. There is no standard amount of time that you have to wait to see a specialist, or standard facility where you have to go for treatment, or even the standard of that treatment. While the NHS does absolutely amazing things, rebuilding broken bodies, saving lives and giving thousands of people second and even third chances to live full, active and healthy lives, some of its basic functions are falling by the wayside. There is a massive shortage of NHS dentists, so much so that in one Kent town more than one hundred people queued around the block after Faversham Smiles said that they would begin accepting NHS patients. There is also a shortage of nurses, midwives, doctors, radiographers, physiotherapists and other specialists. School nurses are a thing of the distant past, pharmacies are closing and cuts to local government services mean that there are gaps in mental health and social support.

If they can afford it, some people will go privately, which is entirely their choice. But, for people who don't have that choice, the delay in seeing a doctor and getting a diagnosis and treatment may literally mean the difference between life and death.

IT'S MY LIFE I CAN RUIN IT IF I WANT TO

So, here's a question. How much responsibility do we or should we take for our own health? If we smoke, drink, eat rubbish and don't do any exercise, does the NHS have the same duty of care to us when we have a heart attack as someone who has been fit, healthy and active? Of course, the answer has to be 'yes', otherwise it wouldn't be universal healthcare, but better targeted prevention measures could save lives, money and resources. Two-thirds of adult Britons are obese or overweight, and obesity, which is the second biggest preventable cause of cancer, costs the NHS around £6.5 billion a year.

The smoking ban has improved health, not just for those who smoked but for those who had to inhale second-hand smoke. Safety belts in cars and drink-driving laws, including the introduction of breathalysers, have saved countless lives. Safer, cleaner places to work have protected countless numbers of people and measures to cut air pollution and to force companies to stop loading food with salt, fat and sugar could have equally positive impacts on health. Yet, politicians who support such interventions are accused of wanting a 'nanny state' or attacking people's freedom (presumably to poison other people with smoke or kill them with cars).

So often, politicians weasel their way out of taking tough decisions by leaving it up to the public or companies to make the 'right' decisions. The sugar tax on soft drinks came into force in 2018 and has been widely regarded as successful, but one has to ask, why were soft drinks manufacturers loading their products with so much sugar in the first place and why did they only change their practice when threatened with tax increases? The salt reduction programme encourages all sectors of the food industry to reduce the amount of salt in foods across more than 100 food groups that contribute the most to people's overall intake. Targets have been set and regularly revised since 2006, but it's still voluntary, despite pressure from the British Heart Foundation and leading medical experts urging the government to make it mandatory.

FOOD FOR THOUGHT

More than half of the typical daily British diet consists of ultra-processed food, more than any other country in Europe. Ultra-processed food, which includes breakfast cereals, ready meals, frozen pizzas, sweets and biscuits, is made by splitting whole foods into oils, fats and sugar then recombining them. This processing degrades the physical structure of foods, while additives such as sweeteners and emulsifiers damage healthy gut bacteria. Ultra-processed foods are usually packed with preservatives and additives, low in nutrients and fibre, often sold as ready-to-eat and are heavily marketed, sometimes as 'healthy' options like protein bars and low-fat yoghurts.

A series of major studies has shown that ultra-processed food significantly increases the risk of high blood pressure, heart disease, diabetes, depression, dementia, strokes and cancer. There are growing calls for ultra-processed food to be treated like tobacco, with restrictions on advertising.

The food supplied in schools and hospitals is notoriously awful, and despite a whole kitchen's worth of celebrity chefs brought in over the years to advise the government, nothing has changed.

In 2023, the latest 'food tsar', Henry Dimbleby, resigned and launched a blistering attack on the government's 'insane' inaction against obesity, criticising ministers who he said were going 'backwards' and had adopted an 'ultra-free-market ideology', which meant that they refused to impose restrictions on the junk food industry.

According to Andy Haldane, a former chief economist of the Bank of England, the biggest problem regarding productivity in this country is illness and that our workforce is not fit.

Actually, we shouldn't need advertising campaigns to tell us what we should all know – we need to eat a balanced diet, drink alcohol in moderation, avoid processed food, not eat too much salt and sugar, keep active, sleep well and have a good social circle. There have been, and will continue to be, all sorts of 'miracle diets', from fasting to only eating protein, to only eating non-protein, and yet we all know that the Mediterranean diet – high in fruit, vegetables, olive oil and with a lifestyle that is less frenetic and more convivial – is probably the healthiest one for us. This is all great if you can afford olive oil and have access to fresh fruit and vegetables, are not reliant on an overpriced corner store with limp lettuce and squidgy bananas, have time to walk or run in the fresh air, access to a park or green space and aren't kept awake by worrying about how to pay the bills, or the noise from the neighbours above and next door.

Jack Monroe is a writer and anti-poverty campaigner who became known for her blog of budget recipes and her experiences of poverty. She successfully campaigned for official statistics that accurately reflected the real impact of increasingly expensive everyday essentials on poorer people and got supermarkets to increase the availability of their own-brand value products. Consumer pressure is extremely powerful, as is the campaigning might of people like Jack Monroe and

Manchester United's Marcus Rashford, both of whom know what real poverty means. They can shame politicians and supermarkets into doing the right thing but they can't fix the NHS.

We watch endless cookery shows on TV and buy glossy recipe books and kitchen gadgets galore but, as a society, we don't seem to think it's important that everyone should be taught how to cook, understand how food gets to the shops or the table and appreciate the value of living well, which is not the same as living in luxury. To return to that Mediterranean diet, it is based on fresh, local produce, no ultra-processed food and, above all, a sense that eating is important, not something to be done on a bus where you wolf down a dubious supermarket wrap.

A LITTLE PRICK

Unless you're unlucky, the chances are that you, like most people, have only had the usual childhood illnesses – a few tumbles, breaks and stitches. It wasn't like that in the past. Childhood illnesses like measles, mumps and rubella (German measles) can be lethal, and for countless young people in bygone days, they were. And even if they didn't kill, they caused life-changing effects. Yet, thanks to the introduction of vaccination programmes, that is not something most families have to worry about today. However, a scandal involving completely false claims about links between the MMR vaccine and autism meant that rates of vaccination fell and cases of measles and rubella started to rise. The man who made those claims, Andrew Wakefield, was struck off the UK medical register and barred from practising medicine in this country. Health experts blamed sections of the media for reporting what turned out to be a total fabrication. Wakefield now lives in the US where he is worshipped by anti-vaxxers.

Polio, tuberculosis and smallpox are almost non-existent now thanks to vaccination programmes, and because health agencies around the world share information about potentially fatal diseases, outbreaks can usually be contained. Cholera often spreads in refugee camps, war and disaster zones through insanitary conditions and contaminated water supplies. HIV/Aids is no longer the death sentence it was in the 1980s when hysteria about the so-called 'gay plague' caused appalling discrimination, fear and stigma.

Interventions to support drug users at pharmacies, drop-in centres and festivals have been criticised, as has the distribution of condoms, which are known to prevent the spread of sexually transmitted diseases. There are some people who seem to think that ignoring something that they don't approve of will make it disappear, and politicians are terrified of upsetting them when actually, from a purely economic point of view, prevention is nearly always cheaper than cure.

Prevention comes in many forms: vaccination or treatment which requires years of dedicated scientific research and funding; or a change in behaviour which we can all do as individuals; and regulation, which is down to government. Was it a nanny state that introduced the polio vaccine or was it a sensible public health intervention? Perhaps the government's failure to act on ultra-processed food is evidence that they'd rather support big business than public health?

BE A SPORT

We were told that the 2012 London Olympics would leave a legacy of a newly energised, physically active UK and that, while few of us were ever going to win medals, we were at least going to get fitter. Yet official figures show that the number of school hours spent on PE has declined since 2013, and before Covid, about a third of children and young people in London, the north-west, the West Midlands, Yorkshire and the Humber were active for, on average, less than thirty minutes a day. It is also not uncommon for sports activities in schools to be contracted out to external suppliers, which often means a focus on football rather than cricket, tennis or athletics.

Spending on council-run sports facilities has decreased by two-thirds in a decade, meaning that leisure centres and sports facilities such as athletics tracks, grass pitches and tennis courts have closed or fallen into disrepair. England has lost almost 400 swimming pools since 2010, with parts of the country that have the greatest health needs losing out the most. Admission charges have also risen, putting regular sporting activities out of reach for millions, thousands of school playing fields have been sold off and built on and dwindling numbers of volunteers have led to a decline in coaching sessions outside schools.

The health gap between the rich and poor has widened, and most of that is simply due to access to, and the affordability of, physical activity, healthy food, clean air and decent housing. Perhaps the best medicine to improve the nation's health is to use your vote to elect politicians who are willing to take on big business, whether that's food manufacturers selling junk or pharmaceutical companies who put profits before patients. You can also support the schools, local authorities and communities who are trying to help.

In 2022/23 1.18 billion prescription items were dispensed in England at a cost of £10.4 billion.

The average life expectancy in the UK is 80.90 years but there are huge differences within the country. In Glasgow, life expectancy is approximately ten years less than in the wealthy London borough of Kensington and Chelsea.

CHAPTER 17

HOUSING

Considering that housing is one of the essentials of life – everyone needs somewhere to live – it comes surprisingly far down the political to-do list. Although politicians pay lip service to it, it rarely becomes a high priority for them.

In fact, it is fair to say it has only reached peak position on the political agenda twice since the Second World War. The first time was immediately after the war when the Labour government launched a huge programme of house building, especially of homes owned by local councils. That led to a great housing drive in which five million new homes were built, all providing accommodation at reasonable rents, as well as being maintained by the council.

The other memorable date was 1979, when Mrs Thatcher became Prime Minister and set about selling off those homes in her Right to Buy scheme. Hundreds of thousands of council houses were flogged off to their tenants at a big discount on the market price. This was great for those who could for the first time in their lives live somewhere they owned, but it proved to be less good for those who didn't get on the Right to Buy bandwagon. Mrs Thatcher refused to let the millions of pounds raked in by local councils be spent on building replacement properties. The consequence was that, today, the number of publicly owned homes is down to 1.6 million council and 2.4 million housing association places (housing associations are not-for-profit organisations which provide social housing).

Every government seems to come to power promising to build large numbers of new homes. At the 2019 general election, the Tories set a target of 300,000 a year, but they have never achieved anything like that. Around 233,000 were finished in 2021/22, which was down from the high point of 243,000 two years earlier. Yet a report by the National Housing Federation estimated that around 340,000 homes are needed every year until 2031 to meet the current demand (and it said that 145,000 of those should be affordable).

Clearly that means the housing shortage is getting worse and will carry on deteriorating. And, of course, almost all of this analysis is about homes for sale. But, despite the talk about providing affordable homes, the reality for millions of people is that they will never be able to afford to buy a place of their own. To them, affordable means that the rent they pay is affordable – and that becomes an even bigger problem if they are forced into private rented properties, whose rents have increased by about 70 per cent. Landlords are not in the property business as a charity; many of them have bought properties which they then rent out and so, naturally, they need to make a profit. If they have taken out a mortgage on the property they have to meet the repayments from the rent they receive. Some people even buy places as their 'pension', to provide them with an income when they retire. Certainly there are unscrupulous landlords who take advantage of their tenants, but others find that what they thought would be a good investment is instead a millstone around their necks, especially when interest rates – and so mortgage repayments – go up.

The problems don't stop there. Many British homes are in a poor state of repair – both owner-occupied and rented. Some landlords are content to let their tenants remain in damp or poorly maintained properties and if the tenants complain, they can kick them out. The demand for somewhere to live is so great that they are confident they can find some other desperate people willing to live in those conditions, just to have a roof over their heads, even if that roof is leaking. Even publicly owned homes can fall into disrepair as councils are so short of money they can't afford to make the necessary improvements. To show how bad things have got, separate inquests found that a two-year-old boy and a 27-year-old man died from respiratory conditions caused by exposure to mould in their homes: and this was not in Victorian Britain, it was in Britain in 2023.

Meanwhile, the number of people sleeping homeless on the streets is rising and the number of families being placed in hostels where they have to live in one room and share a kitchen and bathroom is increasing, while the numbers of people on housing waiting lists reaches record highs. There were 1.21 million households on local authority waiting lists on 31 March 2022.

Not everyone is suffering in the current housing market, though. Those who bought their home years ago have seen its value rise spectacularly. Between 1970 and 2022, UK house prices increased by 441 per cent (and that is allowing for inflation) – far more than wages.

Sometimes house prices do fall – during the financial crisis for example – but then they rocket up again. One reason for the relentless upward rise is that, over the same period, construction fell by 46 per cent, so that the supply of homes was hopelessly inadequate for the growing population.

The average house price in England is now above £300,000 (although it is lower in Wales, Scotland and Northern Ireland). In 1990 it was about £50,000. The average London house price is now well above half a million pounds – a large number broke through the million-pound barrier years ago – putting them beyond the reach of any young people who don't have wealthy parents and a highly paid job.

One of the problems is that in this country, uniquely, property is too often regarded not just as somewhere to call home but as a way to make money, which is fine if you are one of the lucky ones (almost all of them elderly) who own their homes, but is a cause of despair for those who can't get their foot on the first rung of the property ladder.

Another problem is that if the new houses built are too expensive, they aren't going to help young people. Nor will they help if they are built in the wrong places. If they aren't where the jobs and shops and other services are, and are too expensive anyway, they might as well remain unbuilt. They also need to be the right kind of homes. There is little point in providing lots of five-bedroom homes if there is a greater demand for smaller properties for first-time buyers or elderly people living on their own. Nor is there any point in building estates in the middle of the countryside where there are no suitable jobs or shops.

Governments will sometimes set targets for the number of homes they want built and even give fixed numbers to local authorities for their areas, but this is when good intentions run up against the cold hard reality of local politics. For although just about everyone wants more homes built, most people don't want them near where they live. This is known as NIMBYism – Not In My Back Yard – and it results in those well-intentioned targets being watered down and even scrapped. Even if the government doesn't back down, councils can make it very difficult for developers to obtain planning permission so the new homes can is kicked further down the road.

Britain's lack of new homes isn't the only problem. The UK has the oldest housing stock in Europe, and probably the world, so it needs to be looked after properly – and much of it isn't, as maintenance is expensive. This has resulted in a growing number of homes falling into disrepair. Recent figures have shown that 14 per cent of owner-occupied properties do not meet the Decent Homes Standard and neither does a shocking 23 per cent of rented accommodation. The consequence is, that many places remain empty while others are occupied, even though they are unfit to live in. Desperate families are forced to stay in these properties, though, because there is no alternative for them.

Council housing stock has shrunk drastically as the sell-off under the Right to Buy scheme wasn't matched by replacements being built – just a few hundred a year compared with the tens of thousands in the post-war period. For even if councils want to provide homes, government restrictions and a shortage of funds mean that they can't. If you wonder why this is, you could be forgiven for being cynical when you learn that people who own their homes are far more likely to vote Conservative than council-house tenants. (In fact, one Tory council leader, Dame Shirley Porter, was found guilty of wilful misconduct for forcing council tenants out and selling the homes they had been living in.)

One consequence of the housing crisis is that an increasing number of people in their thirties are now forced to live with their parents, hardly something that most of them would choose to do, however much they love them.

If you think all of this sounds really unfair, consider that at the same time, the number of people who have more than one home has shot up: in 2021–22, 2.1 million households reported having at least one second property. Most owners let these out in the private rental sector, but more than a third of them are kept as second homes for weekend or holiday visits, and one in ten households has more than one other home.

So, the great divide in housing is mainly between the old and young. The young may struggle to find somewhere to live, be forced to pay high rents and then worry that they are going to be thrown out of their homes, or they may be forced to live with their parents, and most of them fear they will never have a home of their own. Meanwhile, those lucky enough to have actually clambered onto the bottom rung of the property ladder have seen their mortgage repayments shoot up astronomically as interest rates have rocketed. On the other side of this divide are the mainly older people who own their homes, have paid off their mortgages and seen the value of their property soar.

Is there a better illustration of the effects of older people voting and younger ones not bothering?

CHAPTER 18

IMMIGRATION

When the then Deputy Chairman of the Conservative Party, Lee Anderson MP, told asylum seekers that if they didn't like the idea of temporary accommodation on a barge they could 'fuck off and go back to France', it was a new low in the government's attitude towards immigration. The remark wasn't made off the cuff and off the record: it was in an interview with a national newspaper. Downing Street did not condemn Anderson's comments, nor the language he used. But given the former Home Secretary Suella Braverman's 'dream' of sending asylum seekers to Rwanda and her comments about people who 'possess values which are at odds with our country' as well as 'heightened levels of criminality', it's hardly surprising. This is a far and awful cry from an inscription in Canterbury Cathedral celebrating the protection given to French Huguenots who fled persecution in the seventeenth century. The Huguenots needed a place to worship and a chapel in the cathedral was offered to them where the plaque reads: 'the glorious asylum which England has in all times given to foreigners flying for refuge against oppression and tyranny.'

There is nothing new about people fleeing war, famine and persecution. There is nothing new about people seeking a better life somewhere far from home. There is nothing new about the fear of 'others' and the perception that they threaten our way of life. What is new is the increased vitriol and hatred in the language directed at some of the most desperate people on the planet and that is whipped up by populist politicians, the right-wing media and commentators.

Immigration has become a toxic political football, not just in the UK but across Europe and North America. At the base of the Statue of Liberty, in New York Harbor, are the famous lines: 'Give me your tired, your poor, your huddled masses yearning to breathe free.' Contrast that with President Donald Trump referring to Haiti, El Salvador and African nations as 'shithole countries' and promising to build a 'big, beautiful wall' between the US and Mexico to stop what he described as a flow of illegal immigrants over the border.

By the end of 2016, more than 5 million refugees and migrants had reached Europe after making treacherous journeys from Syria, Iraq, Afghanistan and other countries ravaged by war. Thousands drowned crossing the Mediterranean and thousands more have simply disappeared, including women and unaccompanied children.

The lack of a cohesive policy across Europe that offers safe and legal routes for asylum seekers has led to the rise of anti-immigrant rhetoric and the ascendancy of politicians who spout it, as well as a hardening of policies in frontline countries like Greece, Turkey and Italy where many migrants arrive.

The increasing impact of climate change on food, water and crops will force many thousands more to flee uninhabitable lands, while wars in Gaza, Yemen and Sudan and instability across large swathes of the Middle East will have the same effect. People have always sought, and will continue to seek, asylum and safety, leaving behind everything they know: their homes, their cultures and sometimes their families. Many will risk and lose their lives making dangerous journeys and many more will give their last penny to people smugglers who will put them on overloaded, unstable rubber dinghies with inadequate life jackets and just hope that they make the treacherous sea crossing alive.

There is no doubt that an influx of people, often with complex health, language and other needs, puts enormous pressure on resources that are already stretched. People seeing refugees accessing schools, doctors, hospitals, benefits and housing understandably feel angry, and that's something that various political factions in the UK have tapped into. Taking back control of our borders was one of the pro-Brexit campaign claims and successive Prime Ministers and Home Secretaries have promised and failed to do something about the rise in numbers of migrants crossing the Channel. Rishi Sunak made a pledge to 'Stop the Boats' bringing migrants across from France his 'number-one priority', claiming it was 'the number-one priority of the British people' even though opinion polls showed it was far from that. Yet recent governments have also failed to address the backlog of asylum claims that mean people are stuck in temporary accommodation for months, sometimes years, unable to work, unable to earn and unable to integrate into the UK.

Several surveys in the past few years have shown that people in the UK are far more relaxed about immigration than the Tory government would have us believe. Most people recognise the paradox of the country urgently needing migrants to fill vacancies in hospitality, health, construction and agriculture while thousands of people who could potentially fill some of those vacancies are stuck waiting for their asylum application to be processed. They are also aware of the contrast between the warm welcome given to Ukrainians displaced by the war in their homeland and the outright hostility towards people from Africa and the Middle East. People understand the disconnect between politicians attacking the Archbishop of Canterbury for condemning government policies on immigration and those same people bemoaning the fact that the UK is no longer a predominantly Christian country. While the public are more liberal on immigration, it doesn't mean that they're becoming more lax about the regulations that govern entry to the UK. People expect transparent and fair rules on immigration and for those rules to be enforced.

Instead of addressing the issue of migration, successive governments have come up with schemes that are either absurdly expensive, break international law or are just plain bonkers, like the plan to send migrants 4,000 miles away to Ascension Island, a wild idea that was abandoned just hours after it was announced. The latest bonkers plan was to airlift asylum seekers to Rwanda, although its poor human rights record meant we have to take in their asylum seekers in return. At the time of writing, British taxpayers have handed over £400 million to Rwanda, yet it has not taken in a single refugee. Obviously, we live on a small island where space and resources are limited, but over the centuries we have welcomed people from Uganda, Nazi Germany, fascist Italy, Afghanistan, Ukraine and Syria, escaping tyrants and terror. There are no longer signs in the windows of lodging houses saying 'No Irish, No Blacks, No Dogs', but misinformation, social media and opportunistic politicians are reaching wider audiences with their anti-migrant claims and posturing. It is very convenient for politicians, when so much of the basic infrastructure like housing, health, education and public transport are failing, to blame that on 'other people', particularly when those 'other people' have different-coloured skin, wear different clothes and speak different languages.

Whatever you think about immigration, it is not going to stop and the UK and Europe need to determine how to deal with it humanely and sensibly as wars, dictators, climate change and oppressive regimes continue to force people to leave everything behind in search of a new and more secure life.

Migrants are people. Politicians are people. People vote.

CHAPTER 19

WORK

Work used to follow a simple pattern. You left school and found a job and stayed in that job until you retired at sixty-five, or sixty for women. You might have moved to a different employer, but not many workers changed their career. Life is nothing like that for millions of people today.

The idea of a job for life has disappeared and so has the almost laughable thought that the kind of work someone is doing today is what they will still be doing in ten, let alone thirty, years' time. Look at how many occupations didn't even exist a decade or so ago. Large numbers of people work in computer-related jobs, but there weren't computers until comparatively recently. The same goes for the mobile phone industry.

Then there is public relations. PR hardly existed until the mid-twentieth century. Now all but the smallest company will have a big team, while there are many large organisations which are hired to provide public-relations advice and which, naturally, employ a number of people to give that advice. The same explosion in employment has happened to what is called 'human resources' or HR. Companies used to have someone called the personnel manager whose role was little more than arranging the paperwork around hiring and, sometimes, firing. Now HR is a major industry in its own right. It employs thousands of people and senior HR staff often sit on company boards and are equally as important as other directors and executives.

The nature of work in some industries has completely changed. If you had a job in the tourism or leisure sector before the 1970s it would have mainly involved organising vacations in this country, probably by the seaside. Now there are even more people involved in the industry, but the majority of them deal with foreign trips.

The number of police officers may have decreased, but there are thousands of jobs for traffic wardens, a role which didn't really exist until the 1960s (when it was mockingly immortalised by the Beatles in their song 'Lovely Rita').

The most significant change in employment, however, has been the huge reduction in the number of people working in factories and other 'blue-collar' jobs. Manufacturing has shrunk to a fraction of its former size and although politicians encourage us to 'Buy British', the reality of life today is that consumers want to buy the cheap goods that are made in countries like China, where workers are paid much less than in the UK.

This country used to have huge textiles and cotton industries, mainly based in the north of England, especially in Lancashire. Now, these products come from countries in which labour is not just cheap but where it involves exploiting women and children who are prepared to work long hours for very little pay.

Britain also used to have one of the world's great coal industries. The 1.2 million miners it employed in the 1920s had shrunk to fewer than a quarter of a million by the 1970s, but it was still a thriving industry that provided employment for flourishing communities. Today the number employed in the coal industry is approximately 500: not 500,000, just 500 miners. This isn't just a terrific blow to employment in former mining areas but a social catastrophe for those communities.

Largely as a result of the changing nature of work, the idea of 'jobs for life' has almost disappeared. The careers that young people will enter when they leave school, college or university is not what they will be doing a few years later. Politicians say everyone will have to retrain at some stage and learn to do something which may well be completely different to their current occupation. From the comfort of a politician's office, that might sound reassuring, but the reality for many workers is that they will have to cope with job insecurity.

In the past few years, the government has boasted about having record levels of employment but it never says what type of employment. Much of it is actually part-time or limited hours since Tony Blair's Labour government introduced the national minimum wage which later the Tories cynically renamed the 'national living wage' – although it would be interesting to see how many of them could live on it. Another boast made by the government is that a worker paid that wage will be receiving around £15,000 a year. (Comparison note: an MP's salary was £86,584 per annum as of April 2023.) But that figure assumes someone is employed for thirty-five hours a week, and that is just not happening for huge numbers of workers. There has been a rapid increase in the use of what are known as zero-hours contracts, which means that employees are on call to work when employers need them and employers do not have to give staff work, although employees do not have to work when they are asked. The people who work for companies that insist on these contracts, however, endure an existence in which they don't know where the money is coming from to pay their rent or simply feed themselves. This leads to many of them taking on a second or even a third job.

Of course, employers like zero-hours contracts because they allow them to evade almost all responsibility for the workers who staff their businesses and make their profits while also enabling them to pay the salaries of the managers and directors who, it goes without saying, are employed on a full-time basis. It is sometimes claimed that many workers like zero-hours contracts because it gives them flexibility, but providing part-time work for a student or a parent with childcare responsibilities is not an excuse for imposing job and financial insecurity on those who don't wish to live like that. And, according to the most recent count, there are more than a million of them in the UK, a huge jump of 75 per cent in a decade. Among the companies which use a high proportion of zero-hours contracts are J. D. Wetherspoon, Sports Direct, McDonald's, Burger King, Cineworld and Domino's Pizza. And to prove that they are immune to the class barrier, they have also been used by Buckingham Palace for hiring 350 seasonal workers.

Adding to job uncertainty is the extension of the pension age. It used to be sixty-five for men and sixty for women, but it is now sixty-six for both and extending to sixty-seven in 2034 and sixty-eight in 2044. But even that doesn't fully explain the reality of a working life today. Instead of a job for life, people face the prospect of work for life. There was widespread outrage when the Work and Pensions Secretary, Mel Stride, suggested that people over fifty should go out and get a job delivering takeaways because they need money and they could fill the vacancies created by young Europeans no longer coming to Britain to work since Brexit.

To add to this uncertainty, the use of artificial intelligence (AI) is bound to have an impact on the number of people employed, as well as the kind of jobs that humans, as opposed to machines, will do.

CHAPTER 20

THE ENVIRONMENT
– IT'S EVERYWHERE

When we talk about the environment, it could mean any-thing from the place where we live and our local sur-roundings or the earth as a planet and all its ecosystems of oceans, forests, ice, weather, plants and living creatures.

The air that we breathe, the rain that falls, the heat and light of the sun, the state of the soil, the animals, insects, trees, plants, fish and birds that co-exist or are threatened with extinction, everything is linked and has a direct effect on every living thing on this planet and its future.

Humans are the species that have the most impact on the environment. We are able to make the most significant changes to protect – or damage – the environment, which is why it really matters who we choose to run our government. Decisions, or a lack of them, will have huge implications for generations, and not just here but across the globe.

Growing knowledge and increased media coverage mean that we are all aware of how important the environment is.

You don't have to be a scientist to understand that severe drought or floods will directly affect the availability and price of goods in our shops, whether that's Italian olive oil, Spanish tomatoes or Kentish strawberries. The way we breed and feed animals, how we use water, extract minerals and dispose of rubbish can cause as much havoc and destruction as warfare, on our own doorsteps and thousands of miles away.

Climate change is the single biggest health threat facing humanity. We are already seeing its impact through air pollution, disease, extreme weather events, the displacement of people and increased hunger and poor nutrition in places where people cannot grow or find sufficient food.

Of course there are those who think that climate change doesn't exist, that we can just carry on behaving as we always have and never mind the consequences. It is also quite easy and totally normal to feel completely overwhelmed and frightened by the sense of doom and gloom which makes it so hard to believe that any individual effort we might make is worth bothering about.

In the days before smoking was banned, nicotine addicts would cheerfully say (usually between coughing fits): 'Well, we're all going to die of something', which of course is true, but we knew the dangers of passive smoking, we knew the cost to the NHS of treating smoking-related diseases and we knew that there are less horrible ways to die. So, just like the smoking ban, sometimes governments need to force a change in behaviour, even in the face of opposition. Take single-use plastic carrier bags. People were outraged when charges were introduced on them, but since then, most of us have adopted reusable shopping bags, so there has been a huge reduction in the demand for throwaway ones and a noticeable reduction in litter and waste. There has also been growing consumer pressure on companies to minimise unnecessary packaging or to use biodegradable materials in takeaway food cartons, coffee cups and drinking straws instead. Recycling bins are now more readily available in public places and as part of domestic refuse collections, encouraging many households to organise their rubbish and, perhaps, look at the amount they produce.

So, people can and want to change their behaviour, they just need a nudge in the right direction and to feel like they're not alone. Peer pressure can be very effective. Do you really want to be the only parent sitting outside school with your car engine running when children's posters are asking drivers to switch them off? Do you really want to be the dog owner with no poo bags and even less intention of clearing up after your pet? It's embarrassing to work with someone who throws their takeaway food packaging out of a van window or to have friends who leave the remains of their barbecue on the beach. It is not always easy to challenge antisocial behaviour and to be the first to speak up, but quite often you'll find you're actually not alone.

GOVERNMENT – GOODIES AND BADDIES

Human beings are perfectly capable of changing their behaviour. We have had to adapt in order to survive, but there are times when governments need to get involved and put party politics aside in order to try to solve really big crises. The environment is often the poor relation of government policy. Although politicians talk about protecting the countryside, building cleaner, greener places to live and supporting farmers, as climate activist Greta Thunberg said, all they really do is a lot of 'blah, blah blah'.

Governments have the power to stop water companies pumping raw sewage into our seas and rivers and our precious green space being built on. They can decide to invest in public transport and green energy or support schemes to improve insulation and energy efficiency in our homes. You have every right to ask questions, challenge policies and then, depending on the answers you get – or don't get – decide to use the power of your vote for someone who does care, will make changes and take difficult decisions.

NO ONE SAID IT WOULD BE EASY

Most people recognise that if we're really serious about trying to at least stop, if not reverse, some of the damage that humans have done to the planet, then there are tough choices to make. But, rather like picking up litter on the pavement, too many people expect someone else to do it. Someone else will decide to take fewer flights, use less energy, buy less stuff, make sacrifices and change the way they live while we all simply try to remember which day the recycling should be put out. In the rich western world, we've had our industrial revolutions, flown around the world for work or fun, bought and thrown away cheap clothes, buy cheap household goods because they are disposable, and we expect a constant cornucopia of cheap food while we've exported our waste to other countries and benefitted from the exploitation of their natural resources.

Some people argue that we have no right to tell other people how to live their lives or that they can't have the things we've had, except it's not about telling people what to do, it's about changing our behaviour and using science, our knowledge and expertise to support others. Equally, you could argue that as the richest, most industrialised countries on earth have caused the most damage, then we should take responsibility and make changes to our behaviour.

Almost 190 million people currently live in areas that are expected to be under water by the end of this century because of rising sea levels. Countries like Tuvalu and the Maldives could disappear under the ocean completely.

At least 3.2 billion people are already living with the consequences of land degradation and drought. These are people whose land will become impossible to cultivate and whose homes will become uninhabitable. Crops will also fail more frequently and millions will face food and water shortages. Some people may try to escape to parts of the world less affected by climate change, the places that are already so conflicted about migration and where rich people have become even wealthier by ripping out forests, mining precious minerals and owning food and water supplies.

If we continue as we are, another 16 million square kilometres of land will be degraded by 2050: that's an area the size of South America.

NEVER MIND THE BOLLARDS

People are very quick to protest that their freedom is under attack at the slightest hint of rules such as the smoking ban and on-the-spot fines for littering, speeding and parking restrictions. And, because politicians so desperately want to be liked (and re-elected), they will often back down over enforcing rules, just like the exhausted parents who give in to pester power from children demanding sweets, ice-creams or another piece of plastic crap to play with for five minutes.

There have been furious rows over schemes such as the Ultra Low Emsisson Zone (ULEZ) in London, which charges people who drive vehicles that fail to meet the ULEZ emissions standards. Anger over the introduction of low-traffic neighbourhoods has also seen bollards and planters destroyed and has been described by some Tory MPs as an attack on motorists. According to certain sections of the press, these surreal and heated battles are about the 'rights of motorists', when in actual fact, such schemes are not about drivers but about health.

Nine-year-old Ella Kissi-Debrah died in 2013 from a severe asthma attack. Seven years later, at her inquest, coroner Philip Barlow made the unprecedented ruling that air pollution was a cause of her death. She was exposed to nitrogen dioxide and particulate matter (PM) pollution in excess of national, European and World Health Organization guidelines, most of which came from traffic emissions. You cannot help wondering if the people setting fire to planters and smashing the bollards designed to reduce traffic have ever heard of Ella.

Air pollution is the largest environmental risk to public health. The annual mortality due to human-made air pollution in the UK is roughly equivalent to between 28,000 and 36,000 deaths a year. Air pollution affects everyone exposed to it, from babies in the womb to the elderly, and it causes respiratory conditions like asthma, cardiovascular disease (CVD) and lung cancer.

You might think a responsible government that wanted to improve people's health and save the NHS money might be more willing to support and encourage traffic reduction and the curbing of polluting vehicles instead of seeing an opportunity for a fight between 'ideological' eco zealots and motorists and backing the latter.

WARRIORS, ZEALOTS AND SPOILSPORTS

It's funny how anyone who is committed to environmental causes is often dubbed a 'zealot' who just wants to spoil the fun of ordinary people. Environmentalists have been parodied as bearded, sandal-wearing, lentil-eating fanatics, and when you're struggling to juggle three low-paid jobs to make ends meet and cope with family and other commitments, the last thing you want to hear is some preachy do-gooder telling you to change your behaviour. Plus, the language is sometimes impenetrable. We've gone from global warming to global heating, climate change to climate crisis or emergency, to carbon emissions, greenhouse gas, net zero, particle pollutants, carbon capture, green levies, biodiversity and ecosytems ... and more.

Friends of the Earth, Greenpeace, the World Wildlife Fund (WWF) and other environmental organisations have existed for years and are respected for their knowledge and their contribution to helping shape government policies and strategies in the UK and abroad. Yet some of the tactics used by environmental activist groups like Extinction Rebellion and Just Stop Oil have polarised public opinion by causing huge inconvenience to people trying to get to work, school, hospital or home.

Extinction Rebellion activists have brought London to a standstill, closed roads and bridges, blockaded oil refineries, smashed windows at Barclays bank headquarters and sprayed fake blood over the Treasury. But in 2023 its leaders decided to take a break from acts of civil disobedience in order to make people more sympathetic to their campaign. They had got it spectacularly wrong with a rush-hour protest at Canning Town station in London which ended with an ethnically diverse and largely working-class group of commuters dragging XR protesters from the roof of a tube train. It was a vivid illustration of their failure to engage with local communities and reinforced the image of middle-class activists telling other people how to behave.

If a campaign is to succeed, you have to encourage people to join you, and because climate change and how to deal with it is such a complex issue, it's not a simple 'with us or against us' argument but instead requires sensitivity, nuance and engagement. Protests that look like stunts and a jolly day out for predominantly young white people with a handful of supportive celebrities don't really cut the mustard, they just piss people off. Some people who really do want to do something to fight climate change can't afford a day off work to throw tomato soup at a Van Gogh painting or orange paint over a garden at the Chelsea Flower Show.

There are varying degrees of activism when it comes to environmental issues. Local people protested against the felling of trees in Sheffield and Plymouth. They couldn't save all of them but they used the power of their votes to get rid of local councillors who had permitted the felling, lied to the public and spent huge amounts of money defending the indefensible. Environmentalists and tunnel diggers tried to prevent construction projects and road building and although they didn't entirely succeed in stopping the works, they caused immense disruption and drew public attention to what was going on and the environmental consequences of it.

The message behind protests needs to be clear, and in the case of climate change, it often isn't. 'What do we want? Dunno, but we want it now' doesn't quite work.

Maybe because the whole climate crisis is so enormous and is hurtling towards us at high speed, it's hard to think of what we actually do want politicians to do and what we can do ourselves.

So, maybe it's time to step back and think local. What will be the impact of that planned new housing estate on water supplies, sewage and other waste, on increased traffic, on green space, plants and wildlife? These are all questions that can be raised through local councillors and planning committees but it requires a bit of effort to keep an eye on planning applications, proposals for roads and cycle paths, pedestrianisation and low-traffic schemes and cutting trees, but your support or objection can make an impact and force changes.

It is worth noting that the Green Party enjoyed its best ever local election results in 2023, winning more than 240 seats across England and taking many from the Tories in rural areas, which suggests that those politicians moving away from environmental measures are not entirely in tune with a lot of people who are neither eco-zealots, warriors nor weirdos. They are just people who worry about the future.

NOT JUST POLITICS – CONSUMER POWER

Growing public concern about, and awareness of, climate change has led to questions being raised about sponsorship by, and investment in, fossil fuel firms. There have been organised boycotts of some companies and products, particularly those accused of 'greenwashing', which is when false or misleading claims are made about their environmental credentials to encourage 'green' consumers to buy from them.

The good news is that greenwashing is a relatively easy thing to fight, because UK regulators are getting better at monitoring and punishing companies for spurious environmental claims. In 2022 the Advertising Standards Authority (ASA) called out several high-profile brands for misleading consumers about their green qualifications.

- HSBC – The ASA banned a series of advertisements which promoted the bank's investment in climate-friendly projects. What the ads had forgotten to mention was the fact that HSBC's investments in oil and gas create about 65.3 million tonnes of carbon dioxide per year.
- Innocent juice – Their image is jolly and upbeat, but in 2022 a TV ad promoting recycling and other tactics to prevent climate change was banned because there was no proof to back up the suggestion that drinking Innocent smoothies is better for the environment. Innocent is majority-owned by Coca-Cola, the world's biggest plastic polluter, and the ASA said that Innocent failed to demonstrate how buying their drinks would help consumers have a positive impact on the planet.
- Oatly – Produced a series of ads using selective data about carbon emissions to suggest that oat milk was responsible for less pollution than the meat and dairy industries, which

it may well be, but companies need to be careful about the data they use and how it's presented to consumers.

- The huge global climate crisis conference COP27, held in Egypt in 2022, was sponsored by Coca-Cola and, not surprisingly, was slammed for accepting the deal. This was an illustration of how widespread greenwashing has become and further evidence of how big brands are happy to superficially 'green' their image rather than change their practices.

The power of your spending power, as well as your vote, is enormous, so use it.

PARADOX AND HARD CHOICES

To move away from fossil fuels and instead use solar, wind and wave power to create energy means having to construct wind turbines, power lines to transport energy and fields of solar panels that nobody wants next door to them. It also means increasing our dependence on lithium to power electric vehicles and to store wind and solar power.

Lithium mining requires a lot of water. To extract one tonne of lithium requires about 500,000 litres of water. There needs to be properly regulated environmental safeguards, investment in alternative materials and research into how to make lithium batteries last longer and recycle them properly. Australia, Chile and China produce 90 per cent of the world's lithium and the global lithium market is worth around $8 billion, so there are big bucks at stake, but there is also the paradox of 'clean energy' being produced from 'dirty' lithium mining.

After five years of intensive research by many of the world's most celebrated scientists, they reported to the United Nations Convention to Combat Desertification how land resources such as soil and water are managed. Agricultural activities and global food demand account for 80 per cent of deforestation, 70 per cent of freshwater use, 29 per cent of greenhouse gas emissions and is also the leading cause of biodiversity loss worldwide. The report also noted that 70 per cent of the world's agricultural land is controlled by only 1 per cent of its farms, which are overwhelmingly huge agribusinesses. Simultaneously, subsidies to the value of $700 billion are given to the sector every year, but only 15 per cent of those have a positive impact on either natural capital or biodiversity.

The executive secretary of the UNCCD, Ibrahim Thiaw, said: 'We cannot continue to just take land for granted. We cannot just continue to think that there is enough land out there, that there's enough water and forest and wetlands to destroy, to respond to our insatiable greed ... for food and fibre and animal feed.'

This is not a pretty or cheerful picture, but unlike so many other people around the world, we do have the power to make change. We can choose our political leaders. We can choose where and how to spend our money. And we can choose a better future.

CHAPTER 21

LEFT BEHIND

Politicians often talk about 'left behind' areas and people, invariably promising to do something about it. The idea of 'levelling up' sounded like such a good idea, and indeed billions of pounds have been awarded to projects in various areas around the country. However, councils have to bid for these funds which critics say creates a 'begging bowl' culture and doesn't make up for years of cuts to core funding for local councils and infrastructure like public transport.

So, who and where is 'left behind'? It's not always former industrial towns where big employers have long gone and former factories, wharves and warehouses haven't been transformed into trendy apartments with a host of restaurants and retail outlets. Deprivation, poverty and inequality lurk in some of the most beautiful parts of the country.

COUNTRY LIFE

The feeling that many people perhaps have about the

countryside is that it is lovely to visit there, but less appealing to live in it. What seems idyllic on a beautiful day is considerably less appealing in the depths of a grey, dark, sodden winter. Everywhere is muddy, there is little to no public transport, the internet doesn't work properly and the nearest shop is miles away and has limited and often overpriced goods.

Crammed together during lockdown, many city dwellers longed for space, fresh air and a simpler way of life, but the reality of rural life in Britain is quite different. Westminster and Whitehall focus on towns and cities because that's where most people live, and the media, despite the fact that some organisations have moved out of London, is still very metropolitan in its focus.

Cuts to public transport have hit rural areas particularly hard, forcing people to become dependent on cars, which adds to the cost of living and limits social and economic development, because it's not easy for people who don't drive or have a car to enable them to access healthcare, education, employment, leisure and social activities.

The closures of village schools, pubs, shops and other mainstays of rural communities have increased this isolation factor, alongside the influx of wealthy 'townies' who can afford to run a gas-guzzling vehicle, oil-fired central heating or only pop down at weekends. The lack of affordable housing, poor mobile and broadband connectivity and few job opportunities in rural areas means young people leave to find better jobs, further education or somewhere they can afford to live. That means many rural areas have already crossed the tipping point of having more than 50 retired residents per 100 of working age by 2030.

- *North Norfolk has 63 retired residents per 100 of working age, which is forecast to rise to 70 per 100 by 2026 and 86 per 100 by 2041.*
- *West Dorset has 58 retired residents per 100 working age, which is forecast to rise to 67 per 100 by 2026 and 88 per 100 by 2041.*
- *Rother has 61 retired residents per 100 working age, which is forecast to rise to 69 per 100 by 2026 and 89 per 100 by 2041.*
- *Only 42 per cent of rural residents can receive a 4G signal from every major mobile network operator in their homes.*
- *Rural schools made up 40 per cent of school closures over the past decade, which has doubled since the decade before.*

Agriculture and farming had already changed dramatically because of mechanisation and more sophisticated methods, but after Brexit, uncertainty about new trade and subsidy rules, the inability to recruit seasonal foreign staff to help with fruit picking and the soaring cost of energy has had a devastating impact on many farmers. Some have successfully diversified into hospitality, catering and artisan products. English vineyards have proved a huge success and have now replaced livestock and crops across swathes of the South

East. In some places, local people have manged to buy pubs threatened with closure and turn them into thriving community hubs. But innovation, creativity and community spirit sometimes need a bit of a boost from government through funding, like the Community Ownership Fund, and giving local people more power over their own areas.

WE DO LIKE TO BE BESIDE THE SEASIDE

Many coastal areas also face challenges and have declined over decades as people started to spend their holidays abroad, killing the hotel and guest-house trade. Lots of those former hotels have been cheaply converted into Houses of Multiple Occupation (HMOs) to provide accommodation for people with drug, alcohol or mental health issues that place extra strain on existing local health and other services.

Second-home owners snapping up properties to rent out as Airbnbs have also hollowed out communities where properties are empty for large chunks of the year, making it even harder for local people to find somewhere affordable to live. That makes it difficult to recruit staff who are reliant on patchy and often expensive public transport or have to factor in the cost of fuel to drive to a minimum-wage job. Many local councils in the West Country, the Lake District and other attractive tourist destinations are considering measures to curb second-home owners or at least get them to contribute more to the local economy by paying increased council tax. These sort of decisions need to be made by local people, not policy makers in London.

In some places, regeneration focused on the arts, environment and culture, rather than retail, has helped to revive the fortunes of down-at-heel seaside towns. Margate's Turner Contemporary gallery and the Eden Project Morecambe are just two examples of such success stories. While an upturn in fortunes can be a mixed blessing, pushing house prices up and gentrifying communities, careful and sensitive management of change can boost the local economy, create business and job opportunities and breathe new life into a place which makes it easier to recruit teachers, doctors and other essential workers.

- *21 per cent of people in coastal communities are aged 65 or over, compared with around 18 per cent in non-coastal neighbourhoods.*
- *In 2022, Kent received £4,367 for each primary school pupil and £5,679 for every secondary school child, compared with £6,356 and £8,501 respectively in Hackney in east London.*
- *Of the 8,000 people who move into Blackpool every year, 5,000 are on benefits and 44 per cent are single men.*
- *Blackpool, one of the country's favourite holiday destinations, has the worst life expectancy in the UK.*
- *Rates of mental illness, heart and kidney disease are roughly 10 per cent higher in some coastal areas than the national average.*

- *The Chief Medical Officer's 2021 report discovered there are 14.6 per cent fewer postgraduate medical trainees, 15 per cent fewer consultants and 7.4 per cent fewer nurses per patient in coastal towns compared to the national average.*
- *In Bournemouth the average house price is just under £400,000 and the average pay is £18 an hour.*

CHAPTER 22

TIKTOK, TICK TOCK
– THE DIGITAL DIVIDE

If you think that TikTok is the sound of a clock or a cartoon bomb then you're already on the wrong side of the digital divide and the gap is going to get even wider. But you're not alone: 11.9 million people, or nearly a quarter of the population, do not have the digital skills needed for everyday life in the UK. At least 2.4 million people are still unable to complete a single basic digital task, like connecting to WiFi, using a mouse or browsing a webpage, and 5 million workers will lack basic digital skills by 2030. Added to this, around 1.7 million households have no broadband or mobile internet access.

It is not just a generational issue. There are many reasons why some people aren't online and, as is so often the case, it's the poorest who fare worse and have the most to lose. Just over half of households earning between £6,000 and £10,000 per annum have access to the internet from home compared with 99 per cent of households with an income of more than £40,000. It's not simply a question of affordability. Many people don't feel confident using the internet and digital technology and navigating online services. They are potentially losing out on applying for jobs, benefits training or accessing medical appointments, dealing with their finances, shopping or booking a train ticket. This lack of confidence and the fear of online scams and ID theft is another factor that puts many people off.

JUST CAN'T HACK IT

The assumption is that young people are digitally adept, they live and interact on their phones or through social media, but when it comes to basic computer skills they need when they start work, they're not equipped, despite school ICT classes and various initiatives focused on coding and computer literacy. In 2023, a House of Lords committee found that large numbers of people leaving school lack even the most basic digital skills, which makes them not ready for employment, even though over 80 per cent of all jobs advertised in the UK list digital skills as a key requirement.

The report called for investment in teaching basic digital skills in schools and community-based digital-inclusion hubs where people can go to learn about how to access online services. All of that costs money, but another report by the Centre for Economics and Business Research (CEBR) reckoned that every £1 invested in basic digital skills could generate an overall return of £9.48 by 2032. Filling basic digital skills vacancies would generate an estimated £2.7 billion for UK businesses, plus £586 million in increased worker earnings, and increased tax revenue for the government by as much as £483 million.

But, economics aside, sometimes we just need to interact with a human being, not a chatbot or virtual assistant.

High street banks are closing while more branches and more services are going online, from submitting energy meter readings to ordering groceries, getting a doctor's appointment or applying for a job. Car parks are increasingly pay by phone only and some councils charge more if you pay with cash.

The world of QR codes, passwords and cashless payments can be baffling and frightening for many people, some of whom simply can't manage new technology.

A large amount of school work is now online, but even if internet access is available, some parents don't have the necessary skills to help their children use it.

COVID ACCELERATOR

There is no doubt that the Covid pandemic accelerated the move to online, and for some people it was a new and useful way to keep in contact with friends and family, to attend 'virtual' meetings instead of having to make a trip to the office. The availability of educational and motivational material online really came into its own. People who might not have travelled to debates, meetings and events could join in online, expanding the range of participants and arguably giving some people a voice they'd never had before. Businesses quickly realised they could trade just as well online and save money on renting offices or retail spaces too. But that in turn has added to the already declining high street and services available in towns and cities across the country. Young people starting out in the workplace might have been super-comfortable with working online and using Zoom, Skype or Teams to engage with colleagues, but they've missed out on the networking and casual conversations that help nurture and inform during the working day.

While Covid meant that some adults gained new digital skills and could enjoy the benefits of being online, for others the digital divide has become more entrenched as an increasing number of everyday activities and services have moved online, leaving people left behind digitally and socially excluded.

INEQUALITY

Digital inequality matters because those without access to the internet and the right combination of access, skills, motivation and knowledge are missing out on important areas of the digital world. This doesn't just impact on individual lives, but on families, communities, political processes, democracy, public services and the economic and social health of society in general.

Digital exclusion is another aspect of the inequalities

which run through the social fabric of the UK, creating extra problems for people already experiencing poverty, older people, those living alone and those with impaired vision or hearing.

While the number of households and people without access to the internet at home may be relatively low, every single one of those people is now not able to do something they did before it went online. Companies from Network Rail to energy suppliers, local councils, doctors' surgeries and banks argue that going online is what their customers want, and maybe a lot of them do, but the ones that don't still deserve a service, access to the same information and support. Public libraries usually have computers and online facilities that people can use, but many of these are closing or operate reduced hours because of funding cuts, and there are few staff with the time to train and help people gain confidence on a regular basis.

AI

And then there's AI, or artificial intelligence. Some people argue that AI could have a bigger impact on Britain than the Industrial Revolution, and while much of its potential is good, there are very serious concerns about how it could be used in the wrong hands, challenging personal privacy and national security. How far and how fast any government can go to control AI remains to be seen, but politicians have consistently been behind the curve when it comes to technology, partly because they don't fully understand it, but also because introducing legislation or regulation is an extremely complex and slow process, whereas technology is lightning fast, so regulators are always playing catch-up. It is not as though you can just threaten a company or organisation with a fine or close them down if you don't know where its original source is, and given that politicians and policy makers across the world have struggled to reign in the worst aspects of social media or hold anyone to account , the chances of successfully manging AI seem remote. And what if it's a government that chooses to abuse it for surveillance or monitoring of citizens?

The more dependent we are on technology, the more information we give away about ourselves just to buy something or post a message online, the greater the risk that it might turn round and bite us one day. And it wouldn't take much to screw up banking, telecommunications, air traffic control systems or health data if you were someone with bad intentions.

We cannot put this particular genie back in its box, but we do need to be mindful of how it's used – for us and against us.

CHAPTER 23

JUSTICE

If you believe what some newspapers say about prison, being inside is on a par with holidaying in a five-star hotel. And those same papers, as well as much of the public, think that sentences are too short and those convicted of almost any crime should be banged up for longer.

Of course it is right that the worst criminals should spend a long time behind bars, and some of them should never come out. Although there are occasional mutterings that capital punishment should be brought back – it was abolished in 1969 – there is not much prospect of that ever happening. Though, as we have fretted over elsewhere in this book, so many of the nation's progressive achievements have been reversed, we should never say never.

But with no capital punishment, an extra burden is placed on the prison system, with a growing number of inmates who in the past would have been executed now having to spend much of their lives in jail, some of them until they die. That is one reason that the prison population has doubled since the

1970s. Another is that judges, with little prodding from politicians, decided that some crimes such as armed robbery deserve harsher penalties (a spate of shotgun raids on banks as well as the Great Train Robbery led to the sentences for such crimes increasing from a few years to as many as twenty). The so-called 'war on drugs' criminalises many young people, and the growth of 'county lines' gangs, which use children and young people to move drugs across police and local authority borders, means those who are caught and successfully prosecuted face long jail terms, another burden on the prison system.

But, as the prison population kept increasing, the number of prison places failed to keep pace. Sometimes, politicians or penal reformers would ask what was being done to ensure that when prisoners came out of jail, they did not immediately re-offend and go straight back inside. The answer was: precious little. There was just too much pressure on wardens and the prison system to do more than simply try to keep order.

More than half of those in jail – 57 per cent at the last count – can barely read (those who can have the reading age of an average eleven-year-old) so they struggle to cope with life outside. It is a constant battle to deal with the rising tide of criminality. And it was made much harder when the Tory/Lib Dem coalition government came to power in 2010 and slashed spending on prisons. It was tough enough trying to rehabilitate offenders before, but now it has become almost impossible. Those who run prisons are being asked to do more with less.

The problems in jails are only part of the difficulties British justice faces. The wait to get a case heard in court has doubled since 2019 and the delay between a crime being committed and a court hearing is now well over a year. Obviously part of this is due to the Covid-19 lockdowns, but that isn't the whole story. Once again, budgets have been cut – more than a billion pounds from the Ministry of Justice between 2010 and 2016. Yet even that doesn't explain it all. The pay for the lawyers who prosecute and defend the accused has stood still. Some of them complained that they were working for only a few pounds an hour to appear in a case with significant implications for both accused and victims. In fact, barristers went on strike for several months during 2022 and won an increase in the fees for legal aid cases.

Every day there are worrying reports that cases which have waited for months to be heard have not gone ahead. There is no barrister for the prosecution nor defence and that assumes there is even a judge to hear the case. When there is such a shocking backlog of cases, it is terrible that many courtrooms stand empty. Frankly, it just isn't justice, certainly not the British justice of which we have always been so proud.

PROBATION

Another arm of the justice system which has gone through crisis is the probation service. It has a key role, not just in monitoring offenders after their release from prison and guiding their next steps, but also has to prepare pre-sentence reports on those who have been convicted before a judge passes sentence. Since the service started in the early years of the twentieth century (growing out of the Church of England Temperance Society), probation officers have been an arm of law and order little seen by the public, but no less important for that.

However, in 2014, the then Justice Secretary Chris Grayling, who wreaked havoc at several ministries, decided to privatise 70 per cent of the probation service. It was a ludicrous idea if the quality of the service was to be maintained, as he was warned by those who understood how the system worked, but Grayling was an ideological Tory who would have privatised the air we breathe given half a chance. The result was as predicted: the service became underfunded, understaffed and many of those brought in to replace the experienced officers who were fired to save money were inexperienced and/or unskilled. Some offenders who were supposed to be closely monitored when they were released from prison just disappeared. The private firms had apparently lost them.

In 2019 the government had to accept that the situation was so bad that it ended the contracts of the twenty-one private companies and the service was brought back into the public sector. Those who had warned that this was what would happen were entitled to smugly say they had been proved right, but none of them did because no one could take any satisfaction at what had been done. And besides, the legacy of the Grayling years means there are still too few probation officers, leading to the former Chief Inspector of Probation, Justin Russell, declaring that 'the supervision of people on probation isn't at the level it should be'.

CHAPTER 24

LAW AND ORDER

The British people used to be justifiably proud of their criminal justice system: of the fairness of their courts and, above all, of their police. When we visited other countries we saw gun-toting officers of the law – even traffic cops in some places – but here, ours remained unarmed, except in rare situations. More than that, a policeman (there weren't many policewomen) was approachable. They could always be stopped as they sauntered down the street. There was even a saying: 'If you want to know the time, ask a policeman.' This laidback but effective relationship was possible because we had a system called 'policing by consent' – an unwritten pact between citizens and officers of the law which made for a different relationship than in any other country.

Naturally, that relationship broke down on some occasions, but those were very much the exceptions to the rule. People knew coppers were there to uphold the law and that they had to deal with bad people, but they were part of every community: your friendly neighbourhood bobby. How times have changed.

If you saw a police officer on the street nowadays – as likely as spotting an elephant – you probably wouldn't ask him or her what the time was, or much else. Particularly if you were black – or possibly just if you were young. And you couldn't wander into your local police station – they used to be a fixture in every town until the turn of the century – because it has probably been closed down and the site sold so that houses could be built on it. As for what you would do if your house was burgled, you could try ringing the police, but you would have a long wait before they turned up, IF they turned up.

It is a sad fact of life in twenty-first-century Britain that the forces of law and order have been so run down that we have almost given up hope of receiving the service that we used to take for granted.

Yet law and order remains one of the principal issues that politicians bang on about – and rightly so. Huge numbers of us are affected by crime or know someone who has been: they have been burgled, robbed, mugged, sexually assaulted, physically attacked or defrauded, or their car has been broken into or stolen, or maybe it is their bike which has disappeared. Yet not only is there the possibility that the criminals who committed the offence are not caught, convicted, let alone punished, the chances are that most of the crimes will barely be investigated.

This is not entirely the fault of the police – though they

must share some of the blame – because their resources have been so sharply cut that they are too stretched to cope effectively with crime. After reaching a high of 172,000 officers in 2010, the number of police officers in the UK fell to just 150,000 officers by 2017. Although that trend has reversed, it does show that Boris Johnson's 2019 election pledge to recruit another 20,000 police officers was not as bold as it sounded; all he was doing was replacing the number that had gone. And obviously, new officers have to learn the job while the ones who have left to work in private security or to retire were the experienced core of the service.

This is only part of the collapse of the 'policing by consent' bargain. A number of officers now carry guns, not the ones who are dealing with drunks on a Saturday night, but on certain call-outs, and a significant number of officers are now armed with tasers, which can incapacitate without killing, although there have been several deaths linked to them. Tasers, or conducted energy devices (CEDs) to use their proper classification, were used in 34,276 incidents in the year up to 31 March 2022. A Home Office review found that Black people are four times more likely than white people to be subjected to Tasers. In London, 74 per cent of Taser use involving minors involved those from BME backgrounds. All of which suggests that policing by consent has disappeared.

The creation of what can justifiably be called a police militia was created in the 1980s when a massive police presence was sent to confront striking miners. Officers in combat uniforms, helmets with visors and long batons – launching themselves against strikers had nothing to do with policing by consent and did much to destroy trust which had taken a century to be built up and which will never be restored.

Trust in the police has not only been shattered in former mining communities. A number of terrible crimes committed by serving officers and the exposure of appalling miscarriages of justice caused by police incompetence or worse have destroyed belief among much of the public in the people whose job should be to protect them.

The police's public image has plunged to depths that would not have been thought possible in a more innocent era when a corrupt officer was said to be just one 'bad apple' in an otherwise healthy barrel.

The rape and murder of Sarah Everard by a serving police officer, Wayne Couzens, who had pretended he was arresting her because she had broken Covid-19 lockdown rules, caused widespread shock and outrage, which increased when it was discovered that he had been allowed to continue serving in the force despite being reported for previous sexual offences. And, far from showing remorse for the behaviour of one of their own, when a vigil was held in memory of Sarah, police officers arrested four of the grieving women for breaching Covid regulations.

A long-running scandal was the killing of Daniel Morgan, a private investigator who was found with an axe in his head in a pub car park in 1987. This became the most investigated murder in British history, although most of the six inquiries over more than thirty years were about the police corruption which surrounded the case rather than finding the actual murderer. The killer remains free, as do all the police officers who were involved, and it was only in 2023 that the Met reached a financial settlement worth £2 million with Morgan's family. An official inquiry, which began in 2013, concluded in 2021 that the Met had been 'institutionally corrupt.'

A different, darker side of the police was exposed by the racist murder of Stephen Lawrence, who was stabbed to death by a group of white youths in 1993. The police failed to investigate, even though several local residents provided the names of suspects. Two of the killers were only found guilty of murder and jailed in 2012 after a private prosecution. The others remain free. This scandal led to an official inquiry chaired by the judge Sir William Macpherson, which found that the Metropolitan Police were 'institutionally racist', which was why they had not investigated the murder properly in the first place.

The findings of both the Lawrence and Morgan inquiries that there was something institutionally rotten at the heart of the Metropolitan Police – by far the largest force in the UK – has further undermined its credibility. Yet inadequacies are by no means confined to officers in London. Andrew Malkinson was freed from prison in 2023 after spending seventeen years in jail for a rape he hadn't committed after a disgraceful prosecution by Greater Manchester Police. Police and prosecutors knew in 2007 that new DNA evidence would prove Malkinson's innocence, yet he remained in jail for a further thirteen years. While in 1989, the West Midlands Serious

Crime Squad was disbanded after a string of cases in which innocent people were convicted on suspicious 'evidence' and officers were suspected of misconduct, including falsifying confessions, denying suspects access to solicitors and using torture to secure confessions.

Trust in the police and criminal justice system clearly lies at the heart of an open fair society and the collapse of much of that trust in some British police forces has been shocking. It has particularly affected non-white communities and young people. Yet, too often, politicians just pay lip service to law and order without doing anything positive or relevant to restore the policing system that the country used to be able to rely on.

There are other areas within law and order that are also in a chronic state. There has been a changing pattern of crime and property offences, such as theft, robbery and burglary, which have been overtaken by fraud, particularly online, which has doubled in the past five years. Yet the police have been shockingly slow to react, so that only a few of these crimes are solved. Police officers seem to be content to leave it to banks to sort out or simply to tell victims there is nothing that they can do. Meanwhile, burglary has almost become something the police don't bother with because the chances of them catching the perpetrator are so remote. In summer 2023, it was announced that all burglaries would be investigated. Don't hold your breath, though.

Most shocking of all, however, is the way that sexual offences are dealt with. Dame Vera Baird, the former Victims'

Commissioner, has described reporting rape as 'effectively a lottery'. In 2021, there were 67,125 rape offences recorded, yet the number of completed prosecutions fell from 5,190 in 2016 –17 to 2,409 in 2020–21, and still only half of that number led to a conviction. So, less than 1 per cent of reported rapes led to a conviction. And when you consider that many people don't report being raped because they don't want to relive their experience in a police station and a court, you can see what the likelihood of victims getting justice is.

There is clearly a yawning chasm between the impact of crime and the ability of the police to solve those crimes and bring justice to victims. It is all part of the breakdown in trust in the police and the collapse of policing by consent, which was for so long the envy of the world.

CHAPTER 25

NEWSPAPERS REMAIN TRUE TO TYPE

The decline in newspaper sales has been so swift and dramatic that it makes falling off a cliff look like a gentle flutter downwards. Not so long ago the copies they sold every day, and especially on Sundays, were counted in the millions, and there was barely a household that didn't take at least one. Not anymore. Their circulations can now be numbered in the thousands. But their importance to the political classes has not followed that downward trajectory. On the contrary, they are just as important – some would say even more important – than they ever were.

Politicians have always had a love/hate relationship with the press. They loved it when it was being nice about them and hated it when it wasn't. If you had to choose who was more powerful, it would have to be the newspapers, even though it is actually politicians who make laws and run the country. The number of breakfasts that have been ruined by a Prime Minister, Opposition Leader or Minister opening their paper over the toast and marmalade to read some brutal attack on them or their policies is genuinely countless. Some of them claim they no longer read the papers. Don't believe it. They are fixated on them.

This is also true of other forms of media, particularly television and especially the BBC, but the national newspapers set the debate and the agenda. No television breakfast show is complete without a review of that day's papers. Why? Don't they ever ask themselves if anyone cares? They don't have to because they know there are people who do, especially those who live in Downing Street or work elsewhere in Westminster.

It is important not to think that the papers are behaving worse now than they ever did, just as you shouldn't believe there were never corrupt or lying MPs before, even if today's are taking their behaviour to new highs – or lows, to be more accurate. Almost a century ago, the Prime Minister Stanley Baldwin was under remorseless attack by the *Daily Mail* and *Daily Express*. He hit back with a bruising speech in which he accused the papers of wanting 'power without responsibility – the prerogative of the harlot throughout the ages'.

Baldwin was aiming at the proprietors of those papers, but today's most vituperative attacks on politicians aren't dictated by newspaper bosses – most of whom don't live in this country even though they have such strong views about it – but by editors who know what their papers must say if they want to hold on to their jobs, and woe betide any who don't. When Geordie Greig was appointed editor of the *Daily Mail* in 2018, he made it the UK's bestselling paper; but he

also made it pro-EU and gentler in its attitude to politics –
with the result that he was fired two years later. When the
first referendum was held on the UK's membership of what
was then the common market, every single newspaper – with
the exception of the communist *Morning Star* (circulation
4,000) – urged its readers to vote Yes, which they duly did.
By the time of the 2016 referendum, the balance had swung
the other way. Almost all the papers were now in favour of
leaving Europe – and most had been banging on for years
about the horrors membership brought. They had been printing lies, distortions and scare stories, led by a certain Boris
Johnson in the *Daily Telegraph*. The list of fictions is too long
to mention but the best-known is that the EU was banning
the sale of bendy bananas – a bananas story as anyone who
visited a supermarket or greengrocer's would know, though
people still believed it. It is no wonder, then, that when the
referendum was called, millions of otherwise sensible Britons
had got it into their heads that the European Union was a
crazy, domineering institution.

Newspapers tend to go after politicians rather than organisations, as they are more easily identifiable. *The Sun*, in
an attack on the European Commission in 1990, focused on
its then head, Jacques Delors, with the classic headline: 'Up
Yours Delors'. But usually it is British politicians who receive
the vitriol – and it is relentless.

When Neil Kinnock, a decent man, was leader of the
Labour Party, he was vilified by much of the press. They
called him 'the Welsh windbag', and on the day of the 1992

general election *The Sun* had a huge graphic on its front page of Kinnock's head inside a light-bulb with the headline: 'If Kinnock wins today will the last person to leave Britain please turn out the lights.' Needless to say, many of the paper's (then) near 10 million readers obeyed and the Tories won.

It is not only politicians who can be a target. Anyone or any group can be in their crosshairs when that fits their agenda. In recent years, the papers have painted an extraordinary variety of people or groups as variously nasty, greedy, selfish or uncaring. These have included nurses, doctors, teachers, lawyers and judges, all groups which have at times been lauded for their devotion to those for whom they are responsible but which the papers will turn on when the wind changes. Most extraordinary was how nurses who had been applauded on doorsteps every week during the Covid-19 pandemic were savaged only a few months later for demanding a pay rise to keep pace with inflation.

One of the most shameful front pages was published when the *Daily Mail* denounced three high court judges as 'Enemies of the People' when all they had done was make a legal judgement on the legality of the government's actions over forcing through Brexit legislation without consulting Parliament. This is not something which should be shrugged off as 'just the papers being themselves'. It is really worrying for the future of how this country is run. As we have seen from history, part of the way authoritarian government can creep in is by demeaning the law. And, while newspapers have often been right to criticise governments, at times they are not. The *Daily Mail* certainly wasn't before the Second World War when its owner, Lord Rothermere, wrote articles praising Hitler (with whom he was friends) and the Nazis, and told 'young readers' how they could – and should – join the British Union of Fascists.

From the early 1970s the most dominant paper in the UK was *The Sun*, which was until recently owned by Rupert Murdoch, an American citizen who was born in Australia but whose influence on this country cannot be underestimated. Even though his flagship Sunday paper, the *News of the World*, has closed and sales of *The Sun* are so low that the figures are no longer released, its influence persists, although the most influential now is the *Daily Mail*.

The power of the papers was shown when they survived (with the exception of the *News of the World*) the worst scandal to strike the industry since the invention of the printing press. An investigation into phone hacking began in 2005 when it was discovered that the phones of some celebrities had been hacked into by journalists and private investigators hired by them. As more information drifted out, it blew up into a huge issue. When it was discovered that the *News of the World* had hacked into the voicemail of Milly Dowler, a missing schoolgirl later discovered murdered, the paper was accused of interfering with the investigation into her killing. The more the police probed, the more cases they discovered, leading to a succession of arrests and court cases.

The number of journalists who had been involved in hacking rapidly escalated and led to Murdoch closing the *News of the World* and the police charging dozens of journalists.

However, only two received jail sentences, including the former editor of the *News of the World*, Andy Coulson, who by then had left the paper and gone to work for David Cameron in Downing Street as his communications director.

Other newspapers became embroiled in the scandal, including Mirror Group titles and the *Daily Mail*. At the time of writing, cases are still rumbling on in the courts.

The phone hacking scandal led to David Cameron setting up a public inquiry under the chairmanship of the judge Lord Leveson. After months of hearing evidence and deliberation it made a number of recommendations, including a replacement for the Press Complaints Commission, though this has turned out to be as toothless as the former organisation. There was supposed to be a 'Leveson Two' which was going to investigate other press operations, including the close links between journalists and police, but needless to say this has never happened and it never will; the press is too powerful and politicians too cowed.

For most people, newspapers are far less relevant than they used to be. There are so many other sources of information available, though much of it is as unreliable as some of the newspapers. So the challenge for us as we try to navigate the news and information today is as great, or even greater, than ever. But that does not change how the media affects and sets the political agenda. If some papers decide to keep saying, for example, that immigration is a chronic problem without pointing out that we need to bring in workers for many of our industries – and the NHS – a distorted, unbalanced view will develop. And because those views set the agenda for much of the rest of the media, and certainly for politicians, you can see how a handful of editors can affect the lives of millions, even if few of those millions actually read, let alone buy, their papers.

The number of papers bought from newsagents, super-markets or garages is only part of the story. Newspapers can now be accessed online, and that inflates the number of readers. Some titles can be read free of charge (they make their money by being able to charge for adverts) and the free *Metro* currently has the second largest circulation in the UK.

How people get their news, develop their opinions and act on them is one of the great issues of the age – far more complicated than when you used to buy a paper and knew where you stood with it. That makes it a huge challenge, par-ticularly for younger people, who have more diverse sources of information and tend to be more sceptical about what they are told. But as long as politicians eagerly pore over what particular newspapers are saying and urging them to do, our democracy will remain on shaky foundations.

BALANCE AND BIAS

We live in a democracy where people vote in elections to decide who runs the country, so it's important that we have a free press where journalists can investigate and report news stories without fear of punishment or government intervention.

Without that freedom, journalists wouldn't be able to un-cover and publish the stories that hold politicians to account.

This doesn't, however, mean that governments, the police, banks, MPs, councils, businesses and institutions don't try their best to prevent the media from uncovering things they would rather remain out of the public eye. Sometimes it comes down to leaks, moles and whistleblowers having to alert the press to something that needs investigating.

From Watergate, which brought down US President Richard Nixon, to Partygate, which hastened Boris Johnson's departure as Prime Minister, to the MPs' expenses scandal, revelations about failings in health and social care, the battle for justice for Stephen Lawrence and the victims of the Hillsborough tragedy and many more, it is tireless and rigorous investigations by journalists that have exposed these cases.

WATERGATE, THE *WASHINGTON POST*, 1972

Bob Woodward and Carl Bernstein of the *Washington Post* were behind the famous series of scoops that brought down President Richard Nixon in the Watergate scandal.

MPS' EXPENSES, THE *DAILY TELEGRAPH*, 2009

A team of forty-five *Daily Telegraph* journalists sifted through 1 million pages of information about MPs' expenses. Their scoop led to the end of more than twenty MPs' careers and extensive government reforms, reflecting the power of journalism.

PARTYGATE, 2021

In November 2021, the *Daily Mirror* reported that Downing Street staff held two gatherings in November and December 2020 when the country was under Covid restrictions. This was followed by ITV, *The Guardian*, the *Telegraph* and other news outlets publishing more evidence.

JIMMY SAVILE, 2011

A BBC *Newsnight* investigation into Savile was pulled by the BBC. That decision was revealed by the *Sunday Mirror* and ITV then broadcast its own documentary on the sexual abuse carried out by Savile over decades. In 2013 Scotland Yard labelled the former DJ a prolific and predatory sex offender and revealed that he had committed 214 criminal offences across 28 police forces over 54 years: 73 per cent of his victims were under eighteen.

PHONE HACKING, 2009

The Guardian published the first of what would be a series of articles about the extent of phone hacking at the *News of the World*, which was hacking into the phones of politicians, celebrities, members of the royal family and the general public. It led to the paper's closure, the Leveson Inquiry, and there are still related cases going through the courts.

POST OFFICE HORIZON SCANDAL, 2024

Not all scandals are exposed by journalists. What has been called the worst ever miscarriage of justice in Britain only got mass public attention when it was the subject of a four-part drama series on television.

Towards the end of the last century, the Post Office contracted the information and communications technology company Fujitsu to develop and introduce a computer system, called Horizon, for post offices. Almost from the beginning some subpostmasters complained that it caused problems which made it look like their accounts weren't accurate and they were pocketing money.

The number of those being accused of fiddling thousands of pounds grew fast and so did the number of subpostmasters, usually considered the bulwarks of their communities, who were prosecuted. More than 900 ended up in court although many more – the number is still unknown – pleaded guilty rather than face prosecution. They were all told that the fault must lie with them. There couldn't be anything wrong with Horizon, it was said, as they were the only people to have a problem with it – a complete lie which destroyed their lives. Many lost their homes, their savings and their reputations. Four committed suicide and many died before the scandal was exposed.

As early as 2008, the magazine *Computer Weekly* began to investigate Horizon, followed by *Private Eye*. Various newspapers, as well as the BBC, also looked into what was happening to the subpostmasters. But it was not until January 2024 that the lid was blown off the scandal when ITV ran a four-part drama called *Mr Bates vs The Post Office* – Alan Bates being the leader of the campaign to prove their innocence.

There was, finally, nationwide uproar. The Prime Minister was forced to make a statement to Parliament and the former head of the Post Office, Paula Vennells, handed back the CBE she had been awarded in 2019, even though by then it was known that she had presided over the persecution of hundreds of subpostmasters.

Don't think justice has been done, though. At the time of writing, few victims have received more than minimal compensation for what they have suffered – and, needless to say, not a single Post Office or Fujitsu manager has been prosecuted.

Many people distrust journalists as much as they distrust politicians but, on the whole, the UK press is of a higher standard compared to many other countries and it typically tries to be fair. That is not, however, the same as being unbiased, and it is easy to see how different news outlets have different perspectives on the same story, whether it's about Covid, Brexit, climate change or the royal family.

While there is no law against bias and opinion, when it comes to news coverage, there are basic requirements of impartiality, and it should be free from racism, sexism and bias against particular religious, national or ethnic groups.

Broadcasters are governed by much stricter rules than

newspapers when it comes to balance, which means that different views on an issue must be presented in a fair and equal way.

Impartiality is at the heart of the BBC's remit and is why it remains a trusted source of news around the world. Critics of the corporation say it is too left wing, too 'woke' and London-centric. What makes the news is often determined by what's being reported in the papers, many of which are happy to push culture-war rhetoric whipped up by the government. Yet the BBC is dependent on the government to negotiate the licence fee, which many Tories want scrapped, so the question of impartiality is a daily walk on eggshells.

New TV channels, GB News and Talk TV, which employ Tory MPs as presenters, make no pretence about their right-wing bias and make little attempt to provide balance, which muddies the waters between fact and opinion even more.

In the end, it comes down to us, the viewers, listeners and readers who must make that distinction.

BBC Verify is a new specialist unit of journalists launched in 2023 who fact-check the information broadcast on BBC television and radio, and on its website.

In a democratic society, people need access to different views, arguments and facts, and while you might agree with a TV presenter's opinion, that is not the same as forming your own based on a wide range of information.

Our brains are swamped by misinformation and we live in a time of deep and often bitter political division, so it is more important than ever to have a national broadcaster that is unbiased, balanced and fair. We need to have a space for civilised debate, where people with different opinions can engage with each other and the audience.

The BBC is far from perfect, but it is unique, and during times of crisis or celebration it is where most people go for reliable information. No other country in the world has such a trusted news outlet.

CHAPTER 26

MARCUS, #METOO AND MORE

RASHFORD 1 – GOVERNMENT 0

When the UK was in lockdown and schools were closed, it wasn't only education that some children were deprived of. Those from poor and low-income families who had free school meals suddenly weren't getting them, yet those meals were a lifeline for many families.

The government had provided vouchers for free meals for eligible children over the Easter holidays but then, even though they were giving companies millions, they turned Scrooge to children over the summer break.

Then up stepped an unlikely hero – at least he was an unlikely political leader. He was already a hero to football fans for his exploits for Manchester United and England. Marcus Rashford was a shy, self-effacing 22-year-old who showed he was no more scared to take on the government than he was to take on most defenders.

As a child in a single-parent household, free school

185

dinners had been a life-saver for him. Although he was now a highly paid footballer who would never again have to go to bed hungry or worry about where his next meal was coming from, he didn't forget his past and vowed to do what he could to help children in the same situation. He launched a campaign to get free school meals into the holidays and with his huge social media following, as well as the mainstream media interest he attracted, the pressure on the government to change tack was enormous. It buckled.

This wasn't just a celebrity lending his name to a campaign; he was actually leading it. He was articulate and passionate, he had real-life experience and a very clear message: no child should go hungry because of lockdown. He used his fame and high media profile as a platform for good. Marcus remains committed to, and involved in, anti-poverty food campaigns. He has gone on to launch a scheme to provide deprived children with free books. He also still plays football. Usually rather well.

By contrast, the politicians who had resisted his campaign – Prime Minister Boris Johnson, Health Secretary Matt Hancock and Education Secretary Gavin Williamson – are all gone and aren't even on the subs' bench. It is a wonderful example of the power that one young person can have to change things for the benefit of thousands.

GRETA

It isn't necessary to be famous before you launch a campaign. No one outside her family and neighbourhood had heard of

Greta Thunberg, a fifteen-year-old Swedish school pupil, yet she inspired millions of young people to protest against the lack of action governments were taking on climate change.

She led a series of strikes at schools in Sweden which then spread across 150 countries. While many older people, and particularly politicians, only paid lip service to doing something on climate change, she insisted on action. And she wasn't afraid to speak out bluntly against those who tried to fob her off with platitudes and vague promises.

MALALA

Malala Yousafzai was only eleven when the fanatical Taliban took over her town, Swat, in Pakistan and decreed that girls would not be allowed to go to school, but instead of just accepting that, Malala began to campaign against the ban.

Then, one morning on her way to school, a Taliban terrorist shot her in the head. Her life was miraculously saved and she was brought to England for treatment and to continue her education, eventually going to Oxford University. But she never stopped campaigning for girls in Pakistan and when she was seventeen she became the youngest ever recipient of the Nobel Peace prize in recognition of her fight for girls' education.

Of course, there are other well-known people who use their high public profile to fight for causes they believe in. Jamie Oliver, the chef, has battled for years to improve the quality of school meals, while Gary Lineker, the former England football captain and TV pundit, has not been scared to argue for better treatment for asylum seekers. But Malala and Greta showed that anyone, whatever their age, can spark change if they are determined enough.

What has helped their impact has been the growth of social media. In the past, it would be an uphill struggle to get a campaign off the ground, but nowadays a tweet or Instagram post can snowball and reach hundreds, thousands or even millions of users.

#MeToo became a global phenomenon in 2017 thanks to a tweet by American actor Alyssa Milano in which she encouraged every woman who had been sexually assaulted to reply 'me too' to her original post. The phrase 'Me Too' had been coined a decade earlier by community activist, Tarana Burke, who is widely credited as the founder of the movement. But it was social media that took it to a new level. Within just twenty-four hours of Milano's tweet, Facebook reported more than 12 million reactions, and #MeToo has grown in strength and power across the world, bringing sexual abusers and predators to justice.

Social media has allowed campaigns to have a global impact with a reach and speed beyond the wildest dreams of traditional media platforms like newspapers, magazines, TV and radio.

- *In October 2023, an estimated 4.9 billion people across the world were using social media.*
- *The average person spends about 145 minutes on social media every day – if they carried on over an average life*

> span of 73 years, it would mean they'd spent 5.7 years on social media platforms.
>
> - The most engaging type of content on social media is short-form videos – typically less than a minute long.
> - In 2024 YouTube had 2.7 billion monthly active users and is the second-largest search engine in the world after its parent Google.
> - People in Nigeria spend the most time on social media – three hours and forty-nine minutes a day on average.
> - The most-read newspaper in the UK is the free *Metro*, with just over 950,00 readers a month, followed by the Daily Mail with 770,000.
> - The New York Times *has a worldwide readership of 740,000 paid print subscribers and 8.6 million digital subscribers.*
> - BBC News has around 12 million viewers and Sky News 9.3 million.

It's no surprise then, that, 'influencers' can make considerable amounts of money simply by being online promoting everything from clothes to cleaning tips. What's more, 50 per cent of millennials have more faith in social media influencers' product recommendations than celebrities, and the main reason is, apparently, authenticity. That is one of the biggest challenges of social media, particularly when it comes to politics and democracy.

A report published in 2020 from Oxford University found that governments, public relations firms and political parties are producing misinformation on an industrial scale and are using it as part of their global communication strategy. They spend millions on so-called 'cyber troops', who drown out other voices on social media, and 'citizen influencers', who are recruited to spread specific messages. In doing so, they help to create echo chambers where certain views and opinions are reinforced rather than questioned or debated.

Why would anyone do this? Quite simply, if you can create division and dissent, you can disrupt democracy by feeding people fake news and misinformation, whether it's about climate change or Covid, asylum seekers or free speech. You can build momentum through a thousand clicks or 'likes', even if these come from algorithms and not real people. In turn, that provokes reaction, distraction and disturbance.

If it appears that a huge body of opinion believes that an election was stolen, as in the USA, or that there was no Russian invasion of Ukraine, or that climate change is a fiction, then governments, politicians and the press spend their time heading down dead ends with claims and counter claims and not dealing with real stuff. If it suits them, then some people will see an opportunity to exploit division to cement their own position or power base.

Not that long ago, people's politics and voting intentions were largely influenced by attending public meetings hearing directly from those who wanted their support. There was input – and in some cases pressure – from family, work colleagues and their wider communities, along with newspapers whose power was enormous in the days when people actually read newspapers. Now, most of us get our news and information from a wide range of sources, including social media, websites, podcasts and targeted campaigns. More importantly, anyone with access to a smart phone or a computer can publish their opinions, and that has undoubtedly transformed politics. It's created a virtual public space for opinions, views and campaigns. In countries like Russia, China and parts of the Middle East, there is no free press, just state propaganda, so social media has allowed people (often at great personal risk) to reveal the truth about what is really happening in their countries. However, there are regimes, political parties and other organisations whose intention is to manipulate debate, whether it's about climate change, abortion, immigration or human rights.

Misinformation, spin, lies and deceit have always existed and probably nowhere more so than in politics. Similarly, fake news has been around as long as there's been printing and mass media, but because of the speed, reach and sophistication of social media it is much easier to whip up a 'Twitter storm', knowing that when journalists, politicians and others with a high profile see extreme negative reactions to their posts online they'll have to either back down, keep quiet or face being 'trolled' or 'cancelled'. This makes it easier for journalists to report outrage or praise, even if those posting online aren't actually real people and, if they are, represent a tiny minority of the wider public. Artificial Intelligence (AI) has taken fake news to a whole new level, with 'deep fake' images of people doing or saying things that are completely fabricated.

Social media is here to stay and, ultimately, its users will determine whether it is good or bad for democracy. That means we all need to be vigilant about spotting fake news. There's a certain irony in the fact that young children are being taught how to spot fake news while older people who take social media for granted perhaps don't have the tools to double check, or don't believe that they need to. But, just as with online scams, many sensible, careful people have been caught out and had their identity, credit rating or bank accounts plundered. If we are going to be careful about that part of our lives, shouldn't we also be careful about what we're being told as fact? Look beyond the headlines, they are not the same as the story. Check the date, the author and the sources and, maybe the most challenging, consider your own biases and views: are you just looking for something to reinforce them?

Which takes us to free speech … and more football.

FREE SPEECH AND PROTEST

The Human Rights Act says: 'Everyone has the right to freedom of expression … to hold opinions and to receive and impart information and ideas without interference by public authority and regardless of frontiers.'

So we can say what we like, when we like, to whoever we like? Not exactly. The next bit of the Act goes on: 'The exercise of these freedoms, since it carries with it duties and responsibilities, may be subject to such formalities, conditions, restrictions or penalties as are prescribed by law and are necessary in a democratic society'.

But here's the thing. What happens when a government brings in new laws that curtail free speech and the right to peaceful protest? Controversial changes to the Public Order Act were rushed through Parliament in May 2023, giving police powers to restrict or stop a protest if they believed it could cause 'serious public disorder, serious damage to property, or significant and prolonged disruption to the life of the community.' Four days later, and just hours before the King's Coronation, six anti-monarchy protesters were arrested, held for sixteen hours and released without charge under the new law. The Metropolitan Police expressed 'regret' for the arrests. The UN High Commissioner for Human Rights said the legislation was 'incompatible with the UK's international human rights obligations regarding people's rights to freedom of expression, peaceful assembly and association' and 'wholly unnecessary as UK police already have the powers to act against violent and disruptive demonstrations.'

One of the other bits of that controversial law is that it is now an offence to be 'equipped for locking on', which means carrying an object in public that you are intending to use to attach yourself to another person, or object, or land.

The irony is that the Home Secretary who introduced this law, Suella Braverman, wouldn't even have had the vote if it wasn't for suffragettes who fought such a fierce battle, which included chaining themselves to railings.

LINEKER 1 – BBC 0

When the popular TV sports presenter and former England football captain Gary Lineker used his personal Twitter account to condemn the government's Illegal Migration Bill, he was suspended by the BBC. Fellow BBC presenters refused to appear on a number of shows in solidarity with Lineker and several radio and TV programmes were pulled from the schedule. *Match of the Day* was cut to just twenty minutes of brief highlights of the day's Premier League action with no commentary or studio analysis and even the famous title music was missing. The BBC backed down, and Lineker was reinstated.

There are laws on libel and slander, hate crime, harassment and sending threatening, indecent or offensive messages, but the anonymity that social media provides, the sheer toxicity of so-called debate online and the failure of media platforms to regulate or remove threatening or offensive posts has reached a crisis. The Labour MP Jess Phillips told the Cheltenham Science Festival that she once received 600 rape threats in one night and is threatened with violence and aggression every single day online. Constant online abuse, harassment and threats – not just to parliamentarians but their families as well – have made life in politics unbearable for many.

Two MPs, Jo Cox and David Amess, were murdered in their constituencies. Several MPs have had panic buttons installed in their homes, while others have decided to step down from frontline politics. A healthy democracy cannot afford to lose people who want to do the best for those they represent. Nor should it shut down peaceful protest or vigorous but respectful debate, be that online, in a public meeting, in a TV studio or a lecture theatre. Social media can be a force for good, but an echo chamber of hatred serves no one.

CHAPTER 27

JOHNSON

Sometimes politicians say things they think are true when they aren't, sometimes they say something that is near the truth but a little bit bent, and sometimes they say things they hope will come true, like the promises in election manifestos. Yet rarely – very, very rarely – has there been a politician who has told so many blatant lies as Alexander Boris de Pfeffel Johnson, commonly known simply as Boris.

What makes him particularly unique is that in the House of Commons, where MPs are known as *honourable* members, he uttered such completely incontestable bare-faced lies over and over again. Everyone knew that they were lies, but still, out they came. Did he himself know that they were not true? Who knows. Frankly, he didn't care. For Boris Johnson believed that the normal rules did not apply to him. How can we say that with such assurance? Because we have it on the good authority of one of his schoolmasters at Eton, Martin Hammond, who complained to Johnson's father Stanley about his 17-year-old-son's 'disgracefully cavalier attitude.'

Hammond wrote: 'Boris ... sometimes seems affronted when criticised for what amounts to a gross failure of responsibility (and surprised at the same time that he was not appointed Captain of the school). I think he honestly believes that it is churlish of us not to regard him as an exception, one who should be free of the network of obligation that binds everyone else.'

It was a criticism of which the young Johnson took not the slightest notice. He proceeded to go through life doing precisely what he wanted – in his personal and work life – and getting away with it. When he was sacked from *The Times* for making up quotes from the historian Colin Lucas (his godfather, believe it or not) he sprang on to a job at the *Daily Telegraph*. Posted to Brussels to report on the European Union, he consistently wrote fabricated stories which were published even though the paper's then editor, Max Hastings, subsequently became one of Johnson's harshest critics, calling him 'utterly unfit to be Prime Minister.'

Marrying young did not stop him having a string of affairs which continued throughout his second marriage. When one of them was made public while he had a job in the Tory parliamentary party, he lied to the then leader Michael Howard, who sacked him when he discovered the truth: but even that didn't stop Johnson's progress.

When he was young, Johnson had said he wanted to be 'world king'. As it was, he had to be content with Prime Minister, though few people thought he could get there when he lived such a disreputable, shambolic life and enjoyed a reputation for lying and laziness. Nevertheless, he became an MP, for Henley in 2001, and then was persuaded to run for Mayor of London in 2008. He promised he wouldn't run as an MP when he was mayor, but you know by now what Johnson's promises were worth. So, he found himself back in the Palace of Westminster as an MP again while still writing highly paid columns for the *Daily Telegraph* (£275,000 for a weekly column), which were often highly offensive. In a 2018 column he compared Muslim women wearing burkas to letterboxes.

The crucial moment for Johnson came when he unexpectedly declared that he would be on the Leave side in the referendum on membership of the European Union. When David Cameron resigned as Tory leader and Prime Minister, having lost the referendum, it looked as though Boris's moment had come to step up to the top job. But, at the last moment, his ally Michael Gove announced he was also running for the leadership, Gove then withdrew and Theresa May won the leadership election.

By now, you will have realised that Boris Johnson was like a Whack-a-Mole game and every time he was whacked down he would spring up somewhere else. This time, he sprang up as the Foreign Secretary. In this crucial and sensitive post he attended a NATO summit and, having ditched his security-service minders, he went straight to a wild weekend party hosted by Evgeny Lebedev, whose father, Alexander, was a Russian KGB agent.

The Prime Minister, Theresa May, stood by him, but he

didn't stand by her, and when she hit a bad patch trying to get her Brexit deal through Parliament, he flounced out of her government. May was forced to resign and Johnson was able to achieve his long-standing ambition and move into 10 Downing Street with his latest girlfriend, who he made wife number three, having hurriedly divorced wife number two.

The quickie divorce was followed by the quickie birth of child number six – or was it seven? No one seems to know. Johnson caught Covid-19, was rushed into intensive care in April 2020, but was fit enough later that year to take part in a series of parties at No. 10, which were completely against the strict lockdown rules he had imposed on the country. When the story about the parties broke, Johnson did what you would expect him to do. He lied. He said there were no parties, although photos of parties on 15 May and 13 November were then produced. He said he wasn't at them, even though he – or his body double – could be seen in the pictures. He said that any parties were essential work events, even though his wife and baby and their interior designer were also pictured. And he told these lies in the House of Commons, the most serious offence that can be committed there.

This was only part of the wild rule-breaking that Johnson was up to his neck in. A Tory MP, Owen Paterson, who was a mate of his, had ignored the guidelines on being paid for lobbying. When the Commons came to vote on whether he should be suspended, Johnson ordered his MPs to let him off, which they dutifully did, though few were happy to do it. Then, within days, as furious criticism of the reprieve broke, Johnson told Paterson he had to resign after all. The Tories were furious. They had been made to look utter mugs. But even that wasn't the last fiasco. Johnson had made an MP called Chris Pincher a government whip, in charge of party discipline. Then, Pincher was accused of sexually assaulting two young men at a private members' club. Johnson was asked why he had made this clearly unsuitable person a whip. He said he had no idea that Pincher was like that and he would never have given him the job if he had known. But Johnson's colleagues had finally had enough. They came forward to say they had told the Prime Minister what Pincher was like when he said he wanted to give him the job and Johnson had ignored their warnings, joking: 'Pincher by name, pincher by nature.'

It was the beginning of the end of Boris Johnson as Prime Minister. In the days that followed, fifty-seven of his ministers resigned because they believed he was unfit to be Prime Minister and lead the Conservative Party. He tried to soldier on but he simply did not have enough people left to prop him up. So he finally quit, his last words to the Commons before leaving being: 'Hasta la vista, baby', a quote from *Terminator 2*, which can mean 'see you later.' His dream is apparently not over.

CHAPTER 28

PARTYGATE

There is a principle about dealing with political scandals which never fails to prove correct. It is: it isn't what you have done, it's the cover-up that gets you in the end. That was the lesson of Watergate, when a simple break-in at the Watergate building in Washington ended up with a US President being forced out of office and his closest aides and associates sent to jail. For instead of Richard Nixon saying that a mistake had been made for which he was truly sorry, he lied and lied and kept on lying while the truth slowly and devastatingly slipped out. It was so dramatic and historic that it has led to all subsequent scandals having the word 'gate' fixed to them.

That is how 'Partygate' got its name half a century later, and it was the same principle of the cover-up being the crime that eventually led to Boris Johnson being dragged kicking and screaming out of office. The story first appeared in the *Daily Mirror* in November 2021 when it was revealed that almost a year earlier there had been a series of parties in 10

Downing Street. Normally, of course, there would be nothing unusual in that; in fact, it would be unusual *not* to have Christmas parties in most offices. But the previous year, the country had been in lockdown because of Covid-19. The toughest, most stringent rules had been imposed on British people: an almost total ban on social gatherings, no household mixings, and certainly no parties. And there were to be no – repeat, NO – exceptions to the rules.

The person who made those rules and appeared on television night after night explaining them and insisting that they must be obeyed was the Prime Minister, Boris Johnson. So when the *Mirror* revealed that the Prime Minister's residence was the setting for parties, there was understandable anger. But was it true? Johnson was clear: All rules had been followed. He and his staff were in the clear. And that was that. But it wasn't (as the Watergate principle should have told him).

A few days later, a video showing the Downing Street press secretary, Allegra Stratton, joking with colleagues about parties and laughingly calling them 'business meetings' was leaked to ITV News. Stratton resigned in tears. Johnson blustered on. Then, to show that it wasn't only No. 10 who had been partying while the rest of the country was in lockdown, the Tory candidate for London mayor, Shaun Bailey, was revealed to have been at a drinks party at Conservative headquarters.

It got worse in the new year. It was revealed that there had been a drinks party the previous May in the Downing

Street garden. This time, Johnson could not claim not to have been there as there was a photo of him sitting at one of the tables. But, he said, it was a work meeting, because – and he honestly said this – the garden was 'an extension of the office'. Incredulous critics asked how it was that, if it was a work meeting, his wife, and baby son were all sitting around with wine glasses in front of them. A good question to which there came no answer.

By then, there was national anger at what had been going on around Johnson when the rest of the country was barred from even going to funerals. But it was one particular funeral which led to real outrage. The next revelation was that on 16 April 2021, the night before Queen Elizabeth buried her husband of almost seventy-four years, there had been not one but two parties in Downing Street. Everyone could remember the emotional picture of the Queen sitting on her own at the funeral to observe lockdown rules, and they couldn't help comparing it with the drunken partying that had gone on late into the night in Downing Street, with loud music, aides having sex and the Johnsons' son's garden swing being broken.

But still the Prime Minister insisted he had done nothing wrong. When he was pictured raising a glass at a farewell party for Director of Communications Lee Cain, he said he was simply keeping up morale at a difficult time. Though no one else in the country was allowed to do that, Johnson insisted he could.

He was repeatedly asked in the House of Commons about

these breaches of the Covid rules and every time he denied that he had done anything wrong. He said he hadn't been there, or he didn't know they were happening, or they were just work meetings and essential to the running of his office. There were no exceptions to the tough rules for anyone else, but he thought they didn't apply to him. At one stage he even said that he didn't know that attending a party in Downing Street during lockdown would constitute breaking the rules, but he was the one who designed the rules and explained them to the nation every night on TV. If one person in the country should have understood them, it was him.

When the Labour MP Dawn Butler accused him of lying to the House and the country, all that happened was that she was ejected from the Commons and suspended for the rest of the day while Johnson sailed serenely on. He survived a police investigation which led to him, his wife, his Chancellor, Rishi Sunak, and 123 Downing Street staff receiving fixed penalty notices and fines. He survived a detailed investigation by the senior civil servant Sue Gray, who found that Johnson had attended eight of fifteen events, several of which had been 'notably drunken and rowdy'. There was karaoke at one event and at another someone was sent out to bring back a suitcase full of booze as they had drunk the place dry. Sue Gray uncovered emails inviting staff to parties, so they were obviously not impromptu affairs, and also emails from some officials warning that these gatherings should not take place (clearly these were ignored).

Still, Johnson clung on to power. But under the Watergate

principle, it could not last forever. And so it proved. Even some Tory MPs were getting so exasperated with Johnson that eventually the Commons Privileges Committee was asked to look into his statements to the House. The committee had a majority of Tories on it, but the report it produced was devastating. It found that Johnson had deliberately misled Parliament. Naturally, Johnson, in true Trump style, savagely attacked the committee and accused it of 'prejudice' and of being a 'kangaroo court', but the game was up. He flounced out, leaving his party in a mess and the country in a worse state. His legacy was to be the first British Prime Minister to be fined by the police and the first to be given an unprecedented ninety-day suspension from the House, although he resigned before that could come into effect (no former PM had even had a one-day suspension).

Of course, Johnson should never have allowed a single party or social gathering in Downing Street when he had ordered the rest of the country to stay in isolation. But if he had come clean and grovelled when he was caught out, he would likely have weathered the storm, just as Richard Nixon would have done almost fifty years before if he had been contrite over the Watergate burglary.

CHAPTER 29

LOOK! OVER THERE!

It's the oldest trick in the book and one still used to great effect by magicians, pickpockets and con artists the world over. Distract someone while you nick their wallet, get the audience to focus on something else while you shuffle the deck of cards, saw the lady in half or produce a rabbit from a hat.

Now, some might think it unduly cynical to suggest that the so-called 'culture wars' or the 'war on woke' are exactly the same diversionary tactics increasingly being deployed by politicians. With social media and a complicit media base, it's easy to whip up a storm over gender identity and pronouns, whether footballers should take the knee or whether sex education should be taught in schools. A story doesn't have to be true if you can find people who are outraged, indignant and downright livid about it and that makes it easy for lazy journalists to fill pages or airwaves. While everyone's talking about it, few people are focusing on the serious stuff like jobs, climate change, housing and health which gets sidelined or ignored. For example, some politicians love to stir up a row about, say, 'Rule Britannia' being played at the Last Night of the Proms, gender-neutral toilets or local councils banning Christmas, for while they are doing that, people aren't concentrating on the serious stories which really affect their lives.

Some years ago, a journalist working in Brussels made up stories about the European Union with headlines like: 'Brussels recruits sniffers to ensure that Euro-manure smells the same', 'Threat to British pink sausages' and 'Snails are fish, says EU'. He wrote about the EU's plans to standardise condom sizes and ban prawn cocktail flavour crisps. That journalist was Boris Johnson. He was sacked by *The Times* and courted controversy at the *Daily Telegraph* but went on, as we know, to lead the Brexit campaign and become Prime Minister. Perhaps if sniffer dogs had been used, they'd have rumbled the lies and deceits as a pile of manure.

Once, 'woke' meant to be opposed to racism, but it's become a phrase that has replaced 'political correctness gone mad' and is invariably used in sneering tones by the type of people who think that sexism, racism and homophobia is harmless banter and who think any point of view that doesn't chime with theirs is an attack on free speech (try working that one out).

But there's a more sinister side to these phoney storms that would scarcely rattle an egg cup, because what is happening is sowing division within society, pitting old against young, communities against one another and manufacturing monsters that don't exist. The fake demons of 'health and safety gone mad', 'snowflakes', leftie lawyers and cancel culture are as ludicrous and dangerous as medieval witch hunts or the anti-communist campaign of Senator Joseph McCarthy in 1950s America. When a group of people start pointing 'over there' and manufacturing a threat to 'our way of life', it doesn't take long for something approaching mass hysteria to take hold and the 'threats' to be hunted down and destroyed, be they books, opinions or people.

'I disapprove of what you say, but I will defend to the death your right to say it' is a quote erroneously attributed to the French writer and philosopher, Voltaire but was actually written by his biographer, Evelyn Beatrice Hall.

However, Voltaire did have a few pretty pithy comments which still resonate today: 'Think for yourselves and let others enjoy the privilege to do so too', and: 'I detest what you write, but I would give my life to make it possible for you to continue to write.' (Although there is suspicion that Hall was responsible for this last quote too.)

Most of us would probably say we absolutely believe in free speech, but we would probably also say that that shouldn't mean a free pass to abuse, insult or offend anyone. And it's probably the notion of what is offensive that is where calm heads and clear minds are needed rather than livid, vein-throbbing outrage. If you accidentally tread on some-one's foot, it still physically hurts the same as if it was in-tentional, but if you apologise, most reasonable people will accept that and hobble along. Similarly, some people really don't mean to be offensive; they can feel bewildered and confused by what's inappropriate or offensive and when chal-lenged, they may feel embarrassed or become defensive and even aggressive. Rather than attack their ignorance, wouldn't it be better to try to explain why you feel hurt, offended or threatened?

For instance, you're on a train and there's a family with rau-cous children, playing on devices at full volume. You politely ask if they could turn the sound down, and get a mouthful of abuse. Or maybe you overhear a group of young men making sexist comments while looking at videos on their phones in a pub. Would you say anything? What if you were sitting next to someone watching porn or reading a book you didn't ap-prove of? Would you say something, or snap their image and post it on social media? There are no right or wrong answers. We all have to share often overcrowded spaces sometimes, so we all have to learn to negotiate with people. Most of the time we do it reasonably well, not barging past an elderly person, acknowledging the fellow motorist who let you out, queuing patiently in a shop or simply saying 'please' and 'thank you'.

But what about another scenario: you're at a university where a speaker whose views you don't agree with is an in-vited speaker. Do you call for them to be uninvited, avoid the event, protest at the event, or go and engage in a civilised debate about your differing points of view? Any option apart from the latter is easy, but if we don't engage, we'll never find common ground or a space where we can respectfully disagree. And the more the flames of imaginary culture wars are stoked, the greater the division between us.

Researchers from King's College London reported a huge surge in media coverage mentioning 'culture wars' in recent years, with 808 articles published in UK newspapers talking about culture wars around the world in 2020. Just 106 articles were published in 2015. The number of articles focusing on the existence or character of culture wars in the UK has drastically increased from just 21 in 2015 to 534 in 2020.

Since 2018, the language of 'culture wars' has been a magnet for a wide range of issues: from views on Brexit or the Covid lockdown to the removal of statues, from wearing a poppy or singing 'Rule Britannia' to going vegan. But, apart from race and ethnicity, only tiny minorities of people associate the term 'culture wars' with the kind of issues that have been prominent in media coverage. A Policy Institute survey found that fewer than 1 per cent of people offered responses referencing the Last Night of the Proms, university no-platforming and the removal of statues, for example, while only marginally more people cited the Black Lives Matter movement and issues relating to the trans community or gender identity.

That same research suggests that most people are far less bothered about so-called cancel culture or the war on woke than large sections of the media and some politicians would have us believe. In the same way that we walk past the chap doing tricks for tourists while an accomplice steals their wallets or phones, perhaps we need to treat the culture warriors with the same disinterest, if not outright disdain.

WAR ON WOKE FACTS

McCARTHYISM

Senator Joseph R. McCarthy was a relatively unknown junior senator from Wisconsin until February 1950, when he claimed to have a list of 205 card-carrying Communists employed in the US State Department. He began a vicious campaign against Communism and as Chairman of the Senate Permanent Investigation Subcommittee he held hearings on Communist subversion in America, persecuted innocent people and ruined the reputations and careers of many entertainers, politicians and scholars. Anxious post-war America was ready to accept this new fear of Communism or 'Reds' spread by McCarthy. His accusations were never substantiated, however, and are now considered a frightening example of how effective fear tactics can be.

His campaign has often been compared to a witch-hunt, particularly in Arthur Miller's 1953 play *The Crucible* about the Salem witch trials, which is seen as an allegory for McCarthy's hunt.

WITCH-HUNTS

During the sixteenth and seventeenth centuries, suspicion of witchcraft was at its height. There were trials and executions of suspected witches and anything that could possibly be blamed on witches, was: crop failure; bad weather; sickness. Accusations of witchcraft increased, particularly against poor and older women and cat owners. As fear swept the nation, something had to be done, and so witch-hunters found themselves in great demand and were paid handsomely for bringing witches to trial.

The most famous and ruthless witch-hunter was Matthew Hopkins, who had nineteen suspected witches hanged in Chelmsford in one day. His main method of identifying a witch focused on finding a 'Devil's Mark' on the suspect, which could be a mole or even a flea bite. Hopkins would prick the area with a needle and if the woman felt no pain it was proof that she was guilty, but he used a false needle that would retract into the handle upon pressure, so it was painless.

Another method commonly used was to tie the suspect's left thumb to their right toe and then toss them into water. If they floated, they were guilty. If they didn't, they were innocent but also dead. Oops.

CHAPTER 30

HEROES AND VILLAINS

HARMAN

Harriet Harman has been a high-profile MP since she was first elected to the House if Commons in 1982. She has always been known as a committed feminist who fought for the rights of women in Parliament and the country, and she was the first Minister for Women in 1997. Now she is Mother of the House, the female MP who has served the longest.

The greatest challenge she has had to face came in 2022, when she was propelled into the difficult, and what would prove to be the highly controversial, position of Chair of the Commons Privileges Committee. This committee was charged with investigating the allegations that Boris Johnson, when he was Prime Minister, had repeatedly lied to the House of Commons over Partygate, the series of parties held in No. 10 while the rest of the country was in Covid lockdown.

Lying to the Commons is the most serious offence an MP can commit, it isn't even called lying but 'deliberately misleading the House.' There was no doubting what Johnson had said: he had insisted that he knew nothing about parties, that there were no parties and if there were, he wasn't at them. And there was also no doubting that all those statements were untrue and he had misled MPs. But had he *deliberately* misled them? Johnson insisted he hadn't. And if he hadn't, then he would escape censure.

The chair of the Privileges Committee had been the respected Labour MP Chris Bryant, who immediately said he would stand down as he had openly criticised Johnson and did not want anyone to be able to say that he had made his mind up before the committee had finished its hearings.

It needed another respected, well-established MP to take over this challenging role – and Harriet Harman was chosen. Not only did she have a vast amount of experience but she was acknowledged as being fair and open-minded, even though she had strong political opinions. So the spotlight of history turned on her.

Harman will have known that this was going to be a tough job but even she could hardly have expected what happened when the committee, after listening to evidence and deliberating for more than a year, produced its detailed report. Johnson had been sent a copy in advance of publication so that he could see what had been decided, but he had strict instructions that not a word of it could be released until it was officially given to Parliament. He took no notice of that and issued a furious attack on the committee, which he described as 'a kangaroo court', and on Harriet Harman, who he accused of having driven the procedure according to 'her own political agenda'.

Even by Johnson's standards, these were extraordinary allegations, particularly as the committee had more Tory members than Labour. But far from backing down when outrage at his behaviour exploded, he doubled down on his attacks and his closest allies, including Nadine Dorries and Jacob Rees-Mogg, piled in to add to the vicious criticism.

The committee still had to decide on what penalty it would recommend to the Commons, which would ultimately have to decide Johnson's fate. Throughout these turbulent days, Harriet Harman maintained her dignity, not replying to the vicious attacks on her reputation, but instead focusing on the task of deciding the future of a man who until recently had been the Prime Minister. Their judgment was stark. Johnson was banned from the Commons for nine months, the longest sentence ever handed down to an MP, and had his Parliamentary pass withdrawn. Though by then he had walked, giving up his seat in a fit of pique.

He left Parliament a much-reduced figure, which is saying something about someone whose reputation had already fallen to rock bottom. Harriet Harman emerged with even more admiration and respect from MPs of all parties, including the Conservative MP Laura Farris who paid tribute to Harman in the Commons. At a time when many voters have such little regard for Members of Parliament, Harriet Harman showed that some of them really can act in the best interests not just of Westminster, but of the country.

FARAGE

Which politician has had the most influence on this country in the twenty-first century? A clue: He is not a member of the Conservative or Labour parties and has never been an MP, having been defeated all seven times he has stood for election. He is regularly seen with a pint in one hand and a fag in the other. Have you got it? Yes, it is Nigel Farage.

When he was at Dulwich College, Farage was rumoured to have far-right, some even said fascist, views. After school he went to work in the City of London. He had joined the Conservative Party in 1987 but left a few years later in protest at the government signing the Maastricht Treaty, which would strengthen the UK's ties with Europe. He then became a founding member of UKIP, and was elected as one of their members of the European Parliament in 1999. His outspoken attacks on the EU gave him a public platform that propelled him to the UKIP leadership. Success swiftly followed. In the European Parliament election of 2014, UKIP won twenty-four seats. This was the first time a party other than Labour or Conservative had won the most seats. Then, in the 2015 general election, UKIP replaced the Liberal Democrats as the third most popular party.

Normally, this would not have led to Farage having any particular power, but in 2015 it did, because UKIP's success caused Tory leader David Cameron to panic. Terrified by Farage's popular appeal, he feared that if it continued and grew, it could lead to even more Conservative voters switching allegiance to the new kid on the right-wing block. So Cameron tried to draw their fangs by promising to hold a referendum on the UK's membership of the EU if he won the next general election.

The rest is history. Cameron won and called the referendum, which he unexpectedly lost. In fact, Farage was so sure the result would be different, he made a concession speech at midnight, then had to go on TV first thing in the morning to accept that it had been a victory for the Leave side.

But having achieved what might naturally be recognised as a remarkable achievement in securing what he had been demanding for years and changing the future of this country, Farage had a problem: his reason for being in politics was gone.

He continued to make regular appearances on radio and television, while creating and leading the Brexit Party, which was renamed Reform UK in 2021. He is now the party's Honorary President and has his own television show on GB News. He still has the knack of making headlines, such as when he accused Coutts bank of refusing to let him have an account for political reasons. The fallout from that led to Coutts' boss Dame Alison Rose stepping down and considerable embarrassment for the bank.

His legacy remains undecided, but he played the pivotal role in getting the UK out of the EU and driving the Conservative Party to the right. That entitles him to a place in British history, though not one which many people will envy.

SUE GRAY

Few people in public life are more different than Boris Johnson and Sue Gray. He is the big-mouth, bumbling, lazy politician who yearns to be in the spotlight. She is the quiet, assiduous, back-room civil servant who shuns the glare of publicity. Yet fate made their paths cross at a historic moment of crisis for Britain.

When details of the Partygate scandal broke, the cry went up for there to be an inquiry into Johnson's actions (not that he wanted one). At first, Cabinet Secretary Simon Case, who was Johnson's right-hand man, said he would conduct it, but when it was revealed that he had actually been at one of the parties, he had to step aside.

So who could lead this crucial, sensitive investigation into a serving Prime Minister? It needed someone with special qualities, someone who could command respect and was patently unbiased and unlikely to be influenced by pressure. Not for the first time in her career, the cry went up: Call for Sue Gray!

She had risen near to the top of the civil service by an un-usual route. When her father died while she was at school, she abandoned plans to go to university and joined the civil service instead. She rose steadily upwards but then took time out to run a pub in Northern Ireland with her husband, a country music singer. Sue Gray was certainly unorthodox.

A few years later, she returned to the civil service and her career steadily progressed. She became the go-to person for difficult investigations, including into Deputy Prime Minister Damian Green, for sexual harassment and using office computers to watch pornography, and Chief Whip Andrew Mitchell for calling a police officer in Downing Street a 'pleb'. She didn't flinch from these challenges.

Now she had to investigate Boris Johnson, who was simultaneously being investigated by the police. When Gray's report came out, it was critical but more than fair. The only criticism made of it was that its lack of transparency was too kind to Johnson. Not that he objected to that. It left him free to continue in office. That didn't last long either though. The scandal over Deputy Chief Whip Chris Pincher's bottom-pinching antics once again raised questions over Johnson's judgement as he had appointed Pincher despite his reputation for sexually harassing young men. That finally did for the Prime Minister.

While she was producing her report, Sue Gray's name had been in the news for months, but after it was published she faded back into the shadows. That didn't last long. It was unexpectedly announced that she was leaving the civil service and going to work for Labour leader Sir Keir Starmer as his Chief of Staff – which would put her at the heart of government if he got to Downing Street.

There was uproar, and Johnson's allies launched a furious campaign against her. She was accused of deliberately getting rid of Boris Johnson (not true – her report didn't do that; the Pincher scandal did), of being a Labour supporter (not true – she was scrupulously neutral in her work for the civil service as everyone had previously accepted) and of working with Starmer while she was producing her report (not true – Starmer approached her sometime after the report was published). And the Tories refuse to accept that the woman they now denigrate as being a biased Labour stooge had been hailed by them as scrupulously fair when she produced a report which failed to really condemn Johnson.

So it looks as if the extraordinary Sue Gray story is not over. She has played a key role in Britain's recent political history and not just survived but gone from strength to strength. A woman to be reckoned with.

MICHAEL GOVE

Most of the Tories who were ministers or near the top of the party in the years after the 2010 general election have faded from political view, brooding on the back benches or have left Westminster altogether. But Michael Gove is that rare creature who is still close to the summit of power, still a Cabinet Minister and still a regular government performer on television and radio.

He has achieved this despite having a habit of supporting someone considered to be not just a colleague but a close friend and then stabbing him in the back. Yet somehow, he rises up again. He must be considered invaluable, or a dangerous chameleon. Or perhaps he knows where too many bodies are buried. Whatever the reason, when the long list of discarded Tories is trotted out, Michael Gove's name is not on it.

He is certainly a good performer in interviews. He is not just glib but has developed a masterly technique when being asked a difficult question. With a look of innocence on his face, possibly even appearing wounded at being caught out, he will agree with the interviewer and then say precisely the opposite. It is a breathtaking skill.

His value to the government – or, to be more accurate, governments, as he has served in so many – is wider than that. He has served in several Cabinet roles, the first being Secretary of State for Education in the Tory–Liberal Democrat coalition. Before he took the job, he said he would shake up the schools' curriculum, and he certainly went a long way towards doing that, and more, despite the fierce opposition from teachers' unions, including headteachers. For Gove is not just single-minded, but revels in conflict.

Depending on your point of view, Michael Gove was either the best Education Secretary for decades or a total disaster who undermined the futures of countless children.

He later became Justice Secretary and set about 'reforming' (his word) the judicial system, finding himself facing the wrath of the Criminal Bar Association, which represents barristers. What would have happened next we will never know, as events intervened. And this event was the Brexit referendum.

Gove was a close friend of David Cameron and lived a few

doors down from him in Notting Hill. They were godparents to each other's children, and were. always popping into each other's homes to borrow a pint of milk or some sugar (it was claimed). So Cameron believed he could rely on Gove's support when he called the referendum. Silly David Cameron. Not only did Gove become one of the leading figures in the Leave campaign, he brought in Dominic Cummings, who had worked for him at the Education Department, as the genius who drove the Brexit victory.

When Cameron resigned immediately after the result was declared, the front-runner to succeed him was Boris Johnson, whom Gove had known since they were students together at Oxford. In fact, Gove had been Johnson's campaign manager when he stood as President of the Union and then succeeded him in the role. So it was natural that Gove now led the 'Boris for Premier' campaign. And, it was just as natural for Johnson to be completely deflated when, halfway through the campaign, Gove suddenly announced that he was withdrawing his support because he considered Johnson unfit to be Prime Minister. Johnson instantly withdrew from the leadership race, and Gove then declared *he* was running, although earlier he had said that he didn't have the necessary qualities needed to be PM. He came third in the ballot, so Tory MPs obviously agreed with that judgement.

However, when, two years later, Johnson stood again as leader and won, he let bygones be bygones and put Gove in his Cabinet as Chancellor of the Duchy of Lancaster. Yet even that wasn't the end of this tortuous relationship. When the

Partygate scandal reached its peak, a delegation of ministers met Johnson and told him he should stand down. Gove was not among them. But the Prime Minister only sacked one member of his government. Guess who it was? Yes, that's right, it was Michael Gove, who had instead privately suggested to Johnson that he should quit.

Never mind. When Rishi Sunak became Prime Minister he put Gove back into government in his old role of Levelling Up Secretary. One minister at least appears to have more political lives than a cat.

LIZ TRUSS

Every Prime Minister wants to be able to claim that they have made history, yet none will want to do it in the way that Liz Truss did. She became the shortest-serving Premier in British history. Just forty-nine days after she swept into 10 Downing Street with a personal mission to change the country, she slipped out again to lick the self-inflicted wounds of her brief tenure.

Truss had been an ever-present in government since 2012, only two years after becoming an MP. She held a variety of posts in the Cabinet and was known for something of an earnestly zany style (her speech in support of British cheese is worth having a look at on YouTube if you need a laugh).

When Boris Johnson was forced out of office, she threw her hat into the ring to succeed him and it soon became a contest between her and Rishi Sunak, who was considered to be the better candidate by most commentators. But they weren't the ones deciding. The Tory Party members who had that power handed Truss the keys to No. 10.

Her first move was to appoint her mate Kwasi Kwarteng as the Chancellor of the Exchequer. They had hardly moved into their offices before he introduced what was called a 'mini-Budget', but in its effects it was very much a maxi. Maxi disaster, that is. Kwarteng announced he was introducing drastic economic measures, which he and Truss had been devising over the past few years through their connections with right-wing think tanks. The basic rate of income tax was to be cut and the highest rate abolished completely, giving the rich a fabulous boost. Business taxes would be slashed and a previously announced increase in national insurance – intended to cover the huge cost of funding Covid-19 emergency payments – would be reversed. This was all part of what Truss called her drive towards 'a low-tax economy'. So where was the money for this huge giveaway bonanza for the wealthy coming from? They were going to borrow it, even though that would mean plunging the country into horrific debt.

When Truss had proposed all this during her leadership election campaign, she was warned that the City wouldn't like it, but she brushed aside the warnings. Now they showed they really meant it. The economy suffered severe turbulence as the pound plunged and mortgage lenders dashed to get their money out. Such a cataclysmic disaster was hurtling towards the government that there was only one thing Truss could do: she fired her pal Kwasi. (Though he only found out when the political editor of *The Times* told him he had been sacked while they were flying back from a meeting in the US.)

But that wasn't enough to save her own job. The *Daily Star* newspaper ran a competition to see who would survive longer, Liz Truss or a lettuce. The lettuce won. After forty-nine days, she was out.

CHAPTER 31

TRUMPUTIN

Although this is a book about the UK, there are two leaders from other countries who cannot be left out, because their impact here has been so great. Step forward, Donald Trump, forty-fifth President of the United States, and Vladimir Putin, the President of Russia.

They could also be introduced as someone facing 91 charges in four different criminal cases, including being charged with interfering with elections under laws introduced to prosecute mobsters; and a ruthless despot who has launched a war by invading a neighbouring country and been so corrupt that he may be the richest man in the world.

But it is their impact on this country which concerns us here. Mr Trump has become the leader of a right-wing movement in the States which has created a model for a dangerous form of politics. Facts, truth and reason are irrelevant. No-holds-barred abuse of opponents at every opportunity is essential.

Some of the tactics and actions of the UK Tories are straight out of the Trump playbook. When Boris Johnson became Prime Minister, the President called him 'The England Trump'. Telling untruths comes naturally to both men, but that won't be what he meant.

Putin's involvement in UK politics is both more direct and indirect. Indirect because he would never admit to any, and direct because Russia may have played a key role in the Brexit referendum. The 'Russia report', commissioned by the Intelligence and Security Committee of Parliament to look into that allegation, has been buried, but we know it didn't find Russian involvement because the government told it not to look for any. You might think that smells fishy, but we couldn't possibly comment.

We do know of Boris Johnson's close relationship with Evgeny Lebedev, whose father was a KGB agent and a close associate of Putin, and who Johnson put in the House of Lords. And we know that dogged journalists have suggested that Johnson, a former Foreign Secretary as well as Prime Minister, may have been considered an asset by Putin's Kremlin. Just as we know there are good reasons to think that Donald Trump was an asset – he had several connections to Putin and Russia before he became President.

Since Russia invaded Ukraine, Boris Johnson has been strong in his condemnation of Putin. But the damage had been done by then. In fact, Johnson's – as well as Trump's – connections to the Russian despot may have encouraged the Russian President to believe he would face little opposition from the west when he ordered his troops into Ukraine. Trump still praises Putin and says he likes him because he is a strong leader. ·

One final point. When the UK left the European Union, most countries were horrified at the damage this would do to the world order. Only two leaders of any consequence welcomed Brexit with open arms. They were Donald Trump and Vladimir Putin. 'Nuff said.

ZELENSKY

There used to be a comedy series on TV called *Outnumbered* – featuring two parents having rings run around them by their three children. In one episode, the eldest son had a German exchange student come to stay. They were watching television one evening when the English boy asked the visitor if he liked any British comedians. He says yes and that he likes 'that one with the blond floppy hair …. He sometimes cycles.' The English boy looks puzzled then realises who he is talking about. 'That's not a comedian,' he says. 'That's Boris Johnson. He's the Mayor of London.' 'Yes,' comes the reply. 'Boris Johnson. He plays the Mayor of London. Very funny.'

Fast-forward ten years and that same Boris Johnson was playing the Prime Minister in the same sort of way that people play air guitar. Not so many people were laughing then.

So it's obviously ridiculous to think that someone who makes their name as a clown can become a successful leader of their country. Or is it? In Ukraine, there was a stand-up comedian called Volodymyr Zelensky who got the starring role as the president in a TV comedy series called *Servant of the People*. When real-life presidential elections were due, he stood as a candidate. It seemed like a joke or a publicity stunt, but he won. And then Russia invaded Ukraine and Zelensky became a great wartime leader, an inspiration to his people and respected throughout the world (except in Russia, obviously).

CHAPTER 32

MONARCHY

This book aims to show you that no matter how powerless you may feel, you *can* influence the way the country is run at all sorts of levels. But now it is time to admit that there is one thing you absolutely cannot do anything about, and that is choosing the person who sits on top of our political system.

For it isn't the Prime Minister, who can be kicked out of office at a general election: it is the King.

The constitutional system of the United Kingdom is called The Crown in Parliament, which means the person ultimately in charge (at least, in constitutional theory) is His Majesty King Charles III. As his mother was before him and his son will be after him.

You might think the monarch's job is little more than wearing fancy clothes from centuries ago, including ermine cloaks and crowns, and shuttling between palaces, but he actually has a day job, too.

No Act of Parliament can become law until it has received

royal assent. A new session of Parliament cannot begin until the King has travelled there in the State Coach and read out what 'his' government plans to do, and no one can become Prime Minister until the King has asked him or her to do it.

Of course it is a charade, a complete fiction that pretends the monarch has power. He does all those things because he has to if he wants to hang on to his palaces and privileges. The reality is the opposite. The Prime Minister tells the monarch what he must do and he does it. Or else! If he refused there would be a massive constitutional crisis. Even if the Prime Minister says the King must do something which he knows is wrong, ridiculous or he really doesn't agree with – like Queen Elizabeth II signing the Act to ban fox hunting, which she tacitly supported – he has to bite the bullet and get on with it. If he refused, no one knows what the consequences could be. The abolition of the monarchy, maybe? Or perhaps a cut to, or even withdrawal of, the Sovereign Grant, which is the fortune that taxpayers hand over every year so the King can carry out his official duties and keep on living like … well, a king.

Anyone who has watched the Netflix series *The Crown* will have a good idea of what a soap opera the monarchy is. It has provided the British people with entertainment for centuries, while at the same time also providing constitutional stability. Though there have been times when things got shaky. In 1936, after the death of George VI, his eldest son Edward was going to take over as King, but Edward had fallen madly in love with an American woman called Wallis

Simpson who had not only been married before, but twice before, and was in the process of divorcing her second husband. The Prime Minister, Stanley Baldwin, said marriage to her was not possible if Edward wanted to be King. To which the reply was that he could not sit on the throne 'without the help and support of the woman I love' (that wasn't written by the writers of *The Crown;* he honestly said it in an address on the wireless which is what the radio was called in those days). So, Edward abdicated and went off with Mrs Simpson, both of them spending happy times with their good friend Adolf Hitler, so maybe that was a lucky escape for Britain.

There was a more recent example of how little power the monarch has. In 2019, Boris Johnson told Queen Elizabeth II that Parliament needed to be prorogued – which is suspended, something only she could do – because he wanted to introduce a new legislative agenda. This was a lie. What he really wanted to do was avoid MPs debating his controversial plans for leaving the EU because he thought they would throw them out. Now, the Queen was no fool and she had seven decades of experience, so she probably knew that Johnson was lying, but there was nothing she could do about it; she had to meekly say, 'Certainly, Prime Minister.' Fortunately, the Supreme Court stepped in and all eleven justices on it unanimously proclaimed the prorogation to be unlawful. Whether the Queen was secretly delighted that Johnson had got his comeuppance or furious that she had been made to look weak and powerless is anyone's guess.

When Elizabeth died after seventy years on the throne,

there was no election for her successor. Her eldest son, Charles, got the job. He had been waiting for it for half a century, the longest apprenticeship in history. And when he passes on, we know who the next one on the throne will be: arise, King William V! Considering how long monarchs live nowadays, it will be not far off the twenty-second century when William is succeeded by King George VII, his eldest son. Incidentally, the reason none of the next few monarchs will be a queen is that the eldest children are male, but until 2011 it didn't matter if the eldest child was a son or a daughter, no woman could become monarch if she had an older brother; a son who was younger than her would take precedence. (Elizabeth I only became Queen because her father Henry's son was dead.) So if Charles had died before he had produced an heir, we would now have on our throne not Queen Anne but King Andrew, a narrow escape.

As mentioned above, the monarch – who is one of the richest people in the country – still receives money from British taxpayers, known as the Sovereign Grant. He is not affected by austerity or public-sector pay freezes. Even without union representation he can get huge rises. From 2025 he will receive an income of £125 million, a 45 per cent boost from public funding. Nice work if you can get it, but you won't get it unless you are the monarch's eldest child.

CHAPTER 33

PUB QUIZ PARLIAMENTARY FACTS

POTTED HISTORY

Until the middle of the thirteenth century, the monarchs of England occasionally summoned knights, barons and bishops to their palace at Westminster for what were early versions of away-day sessions. The barons were supposed to represent the views of the people in their shires or towns, but not go as far as disagreeing with the King, though they did sometimes. So Parliament was divided into two groups – the Commoners (from commune, not common) and the Lords, which is pretty much what we have now.

By the middle of the seventeenth century, England had had a civil war, executed a king (Charles I in 1642) and Parliament had won. Not for long, though. Eighteen years later, Charles's son, imaginatively called Charles II, was restored to the throne.

In those days, it was rich landowners and their sons who became MPs, but gradually, the people who were elected came from different backgrounds. Political parties were created – the Whigs, who later became the Liberal Party, and the Tories, who later became … well, Tories, although they are sometimes referred to as Conservatives. In 1900, a new party was created by the trades union movement: the Labour Party.

It was still only men who had the vote – and most of them didn't until 1918, when all men over twenty-one could vote. It was 1928 before women in the UK had the same voting rights as men, more than thirty years after women in New Zealand won the right.

FACTS

The UK Parliament is made up of two chambers or 'Houses': the House of Commons and the House of Lords.

- *The House of Commons has 650 Members of Parliament (MPs). Each MP represents a part of the UK called a 'constituency' or 'seat'. The political party with the most MPs in the House of Commons forms the government. The government propose new laws and raises issues for Parliament to debate. It also puts into action. the decisions made by Parliament.*
- *The House of Lords has around 780 unelected members who scrutinise the work of the House of Commons. Before 1999 the Lords was mostly made up of men who had inherited their titles, but reforms meant that the majority of members are now 'life peers', so that the title isn't passed on. They should be appointed for their knowledge or experience in*

a particular field. However, some are 'rewarded' by Prime Ministers for sycophancy or keeping secrets, or perhaps donating large sums of money to a political party.

- When a bill is announced for the first time (usually in the House of Commons) it is called the First Reading. At the Second Reading, which usually happens two weeks later, MPs get a chance to debate and discuss its general principles. They then vote to decide whether the bill should be discussed further or simply rejected.

- If it's not thrown out at this stage, the bill is given to a group of MPs in a committee to examine the details and suggest changes. The committee then reports back to the House to give all MPs the chance to suggest further amendments. This is the Report Stage.

- The Third Reading is technically the final chance for MPs to debate whether or not to pass the bill after all amendments have been made, but in practice it is a formality and it is very rare for meaningful debates to take place. However, once the Commons has agreed on it, the bill is passed to the House of Lords for a second opinion. This is where experts in the Lords can influence things based on their knowledge, and experience in, science, law, foreign affairs, military matters, medicine and other fields. If the Lords agree with the House of Commons, the bill becomes a law. If they make amendments, they send the bill back to the Commons until both Houses agree, but it is only after the monarch has given his seal of approval that the bill finally becomes a fully fledged law or Act of Parliament. This is called the royal assent.

- *Media coverage of parliamentary proceedings has mainly been reduced to reports on the weekly sparring at Prime Minister's Questions, which is usually a meaningless shouting match. If you really want to know and understand what's happening in Parliament, you'll learn more from the select committees which, like all parliamentary proceedings, are televised and shown on the BBC Parliament Channel. Select committees are made up of MPs from all parties and their job is to scrutinise and challenge government policy.*

- *At a general election you have one vote to choose a candidate to represent your constituency in the House of Commons. Most candidates are from a political party but there can also be independent candidates. The leader of the party with the most MPs is asked by the monarch to become Prime Minister and to form a government. The leader of the party with the second highest number of MPs becomes the Leader of the Opposition. And then they spend every Wednesday lunchtime shouting at each other across the floor of the House of Commons until the next election.*

- *The most important people speak from the despatch boxes, the wooden boxes on the table between the government and opposition parties which are used as lecterns by the Prime Minister, ministers and the Leader of the Opposition and shadow ministers. It is why we talk of someone's performance 'at the despatch box'. Bibles are kept in the boxes and other bits and bobs used for the swearing-in of new MPs.*

- *There is also the mace on the table in the middle of the Chamber. It represents the monarch's authority in Parliament and*

> *without it, Parliament cannot meet or pass laws. It is carried in and out of the Commons and Lords chambers in a procession at the beginning and end of each day.*
>
> - *MPs who dare to touch the mace are in big trouble. Michael, now Lord, Heseltine famously seized the mace after a particularly heated debate in 1976. In 2009, Labour MP John McDonnell was so furious about the decision to go ahead with a third runway at Heathrow Airport, he picked up the mace and was suspended from Parliament for five days. More recently, Labour's Lloyd Russell-Moyle grabbed the mace in protest and held it up in the centre of the Chamber.*

You may wonder what any of this has got to do with our daily lives, but lots of places have rituals and customs that seem completely random. Churches, mosques, synagogues, schools, courts and anything to do with royalty. These are usually something dating way back but all to do with registering the fact that you are in a serious or special place – and some people just like dressing up.

AND THE WINNER IS...

MPs are elected to the UK Parliament under what is called the first-past-the-post system. It means that the candidate who gets the most votes, wins, even if they only win by one and even if the other candidates get more votes together than the one who eventually becomes the MP. This system, which is followed in few other places in the world, is often criticised for not being truly representative, because very often more people *don't* vote for the party that wins. And not only win, but achieve a large majority.

In 2019, the Conservatives received an overall majority of eighty seats on a vote share of only 43.6 per cent, and the number of seats they won went up by forty-eight over the previous general election, although their share of the vote increased by just 1.2 per cent. So, what happens to the votes cast for losing candidates? Nothing. They are ignored.

Here are some facts and figures about the 2019 general election:

- More than 22 million votes (70.8 per cent of those cast) were ignored because they went to non-elected candidates or were surplus to what the winning candidate needed to win the seat.
- The number of Conservative votes cast worked out at 38,264 per MP, while the Greens won 864,743 votes but got only one MP.
- The Liberal Democrats increased their vote share by 4.2 per cent but lost a seat in Parliament.
- Of the 650 seats, 67 were won by a margin of 5 per cent or less of the votes cast. Twelve seats were won with majorities of fewer than 1 per cent of valid votes cast.
- About 45 per cent of voters ended up with a representative they did not vote for. That is roughly 14.5 million disenfranchised voters.

Nigel Farage and UKIP never won a seat in a general election despite his high public profile and the fact that the threat of UKIP taking Conservative seats had some influence on David Cameron's decision to hold the 2016 referendum that resulted in Brexit. Likewise, despite an increase in local councillors, heightened public awareness and support for environmental issues, Caroline Lucas remained the Green Party's only MP. No wonder people often feel their vote doesn't count or it's not worth bothering. The arguments for Proportional Representation (PR) are that it could lead to a higher turnout at the polls, voters would feel more engaged with the democratic process and candidates would need to appeal to a much larger section of the public and focus more on local issues rather than just targeting a tiny proportion of swing voters.

But voting habits have changed and people have got more canny about how to use their vote. They mark their X against the candidate they think is most likely to beat the one they really don't want to win, which is often the sitting MP. This is called tactical voting. Students, who can register either at their home or where they are studying, can have a huge impact on elections – that is widely credited for the historic Labour win in Canterbury in 2017, when the party scraped home by just 187 votes. The Tories had held the seat ever since it was created. Quite often, people vote differently in local elections than in general elections. That might be because of local issues or it could be that they want to send a protest message to the government. In the local elections, councils and councillors often lose or gain power by just a handful of votes. So votes can and do make a difference even under our imperfect system.

TACTICAL VOTING

Here is an example from the imaginary constituency of Sunshine-on-Sea, where there are three candidates: Green, Brown and Pink. Ms. Brown gets 40 per cent of the votes, while Mr Green gets 35 per cent and Mrs Pink just 25 per cent. So Ms. Brown becomes the MP although 60 per cent of her constituents wanted one of the other two. By the vote against her being split, she was able to come through the middle to victory.

Now, consider what would have happened if the backers of Mr Green and Mrs Pink had done a deal so only one of them stood. That candidate may well have won – at least they would have done if enough of Mrs Pink's supporters could have been persuaded to throw their weight behind Mr Green. Then, instead of Ms. Brown going triumphantly to Westminster, Mr Green would have become the MP. Of course, Mrs Pink's supporters, having lent their votes to Mr Green, would not have got their first-choice MP, but they would have succeeded in beating Ms. Brown. This is known as tactical voting.

It has been talked about for years by political sophisticates but rarely got anywhere, except in by-elections when voters seem more focused on getting rid of certain candidates. But there seems to be more of an appetite for it recently, perhaps because one party has been in power for so long, Or maybe voters

---

are getting more sophisticated and not just going to the polling booth and marking an X for the candidate or party they most want. And if enough people vote tactically, they can succeed not just in changing the result in their constituency, but nationally.

This could have historic consequences. The Conservatives are known as the most successful political party of the past century, winning more general elections and forming the government for longer than any other party. But psephologists – people who study elections – say that there have almost always been more people who didn't vote for the Tories than did. It was just that the combined support for other parties had been split between Labour, the Liberal Democrats and the Greens. Of course, this is a simplistic way to look at it: not everyone who, say, wants to vote Green will lend their vote to Labour or who wants to vote Labour will lend their vote to the Liberal Democrats. But if enough of them do, and do it effectively, it is possible to change the result.

Naturally, if there was a different voting system in which every vote counted, tactical voting wouldn't be necessary. But as long as it is, it means that voters should think even harder where they will place that precious X on the ballot paper.

WHAT'S THE ALTERNATIVE?

'Democracy is the worst form of Government except for all those other forms that have been tried from time to time.' These are the words of Winston Churchill, spoken in 1947 when he'd been voted out of office months after the end of the Second World War, a war that was a battle for democracy across Europe.

Britain and America are very keen to promote democracy as the best way to run a country in other parts of the world, as it gives people the right to vote for those they want to run their country. Of course, we know that many nations simply pay lip service to democracy, with threats to opposition politicians, media censorship, corruption and rigged elections. We also know that democracy in our own country, and the USA, is found wanting, so Churchill was right in saying that democracy is not perfect.

We have seen the rise of 'populist' politicians like Donald Trump, Boris Johnson, Nigel Farage, Macron in France, Meloni in Italy, Erdoğan in Turkey and Orbán in Hungary. They have gained power and influence through tapping into the feelings of ordinary, hard-working people who feel like they have been ignored and left behind by a liberal elite who they believe control mainstream politics. Populist politicians have an appeal of authenticity. They are seen as just like us, the sort of person you'd feel comfortable hanging out with, straight-talking and a bit outrageous. We know all too well what happens when a leader who might be fun in the pub has to deal with the hard stuff like Covid or Brexit or social care and education: they can't. We have also seen how populists, like Trump, refuse to accept election results. We've seen populists turn on anyone who disagrees with them and are happy to stoke conspiracy theories and culture wars by increasing the fear of 'others', usually immigrants, ethnic and religious minorities or LGBTQ+ people.

It is only human to breathe a sigh of relief when you discover you're not alone, there are others out there who feel like you do, who have the same questions, concerns and views – views that previously, you might have been hesitant to share for fear of being accused of racism, homophobia, misogyny or stupidity. At last, you have a voice, along with others like you. Sadly, those voices too often become a baying mob, as we saw when supporters of former President Donald Trump stormed Congress in 2021 to try to stop Joe Biden's election victory being certified. Populists generally aren't very good at detail or long-term thinking about how to actually run a country and what makes it function – the boring stuff like transport, education, health, budgets, housing, employment, food and water supplies. They have found it much easier to create phoney threats and conflict about different cultures, beliefs and behaviours, because if you can control a population by making them fearful, you then have an awful lot of power and, because people are too busy being scared, they're not going to ask difficult questions about the things that really matter.

If leaders have that sort of power, they can exercise it even more by controlling who gets to vote, the right to protest, free speech and media. Once that happens, it's very hard to get rid of them, so maybe best not to let them get there in the first place.

Democracy and politics in practice is not just what

happens in Parliament, council chambers, Senate buildings and during elections. It's how people with different views can live together relatively peacefully. A verbal punch-up has got to be far better than physical ones. When ideas and opinions can be freely shared and debated, people are more willing to compromise, to see another point of view, listen to a different voice, and then we are on the way to a civil society that is tolerant and fair. But that's a fragile thing that needs protecting and nurturing. To paraphrase the ancient Greek philosopher Plato 'the price good people pay for indifference to public affairs is to be ruled by evil men.'

FACTS

Democracy is when people have a say in the governing of their country, usually by electing people to represent them in a Parliament and make laws on their behalf.

Other forms of government include:

- *Monarchy – the monarch is the head of state and supreme ruler*
- *Dictatorship – the rule by one person with supreme authority*
- *Oligarchy – a country governed by a small group of people*
- *Theocracy – a country governed according to religious rules, usually by ordained members of that religion (clergy)*
- *One-party rule – no other political parties are allowed*

CHAPTER 34

THE UNIONS

Most of us will spend more of our lives working than not. Indeed, we are all being expected to work longer, well into what was once considered old age. Few of us will stay in the same job for life, many of us will have a mixture of part-time, freelance or full-time employment and periods of no work.

Jobs and the workplace are changing at a rapid pace, which was accelerated by Covid-19. The pandemic forced those who could to work from home and many still haven't returned to the office full-time. Obviously if you're a surgeon, a cleaner, firefighter or mechanic, you can't do your job from home or on Zoom. But Covid forced change on many organisations, people decided they wanted more flexibility at work and weren't prepared to spend time and money on commuting just to be present in a workplace when their jobs and meetings could be done virtually. Employers realised that they could in fact trust people to do their jobs from home, attend virtual meetings and, in many cases, have recognised that flexible hours are as attractive to employees as good salaries.

More jobs will be lost to technology as AI takes on roles previously performed by humans, and zero-hours contracts are here to stay. So, you might ask, who needs a trade union?

Work works like this.

You sell your labour and skills in return for money. Sounds pretty straightforward, yet political theorists, social campaigners and philosophers have agonised for centuries over the relationship between the employee and the employer.

It doesn't matter whether you're a City banker or doing three part-time jobs cleaning, you work in a kitchen or a care home, usually you work because you need money to live. So, you're dependent on your employer, who can bully, threaten or exploit you.

One thing stands between workers being trampled all over, as they were for centuries, and a working life that provides them with at least a modicum of dignity, decent conditions and reasonable pay. That is the trade unions, which give ordinary people the chance to prevent bosses from treating their employees badly.

Unions have fought for better working conditions in factories, farms, hospitals, call centres, schools, building sites and government offices. They have campaigned for workers' rights to sick pay and maternity leave, paid holidays and safety at work. They have a long and proud history of providing education to people who otherwise would have had no access to books and learning resources.

They have fought for equal rights, reasonable working hours and stood up to bullies who wanted to deny workers these rights. Having battled to extend the franchise, unions created a political party that working people could vote for, the Labour Party, in case that description of Labour has passed you by.

Sure, when airport baggage handlers go on strike during the summer-holiday period, it's infuriating for anyone caught up in delays and chaos that affect their hard-earned holiday. The same goes for strikes affecting public transport, postal services and bin collections.

Inevitably, some parts of the media attack the unions for being selfish, overpaid Communist sympathisers who resist change and enjoy causing mayhem and misery for other people. Older people will remember when the unions had much more clout, millions more members and almost brought the country to its knees with lengthy strikes at factories, coal mines, ports and council offices. Some sections of the media like to recreate the hysterical outrage at the actions of the so-called 'union barons' who could make governments quake, Prime Ministers fume and bend the country to their bidding.

But that narrative was harder to use when, in 2022, nurses voted for strike action for the first time in the Royal College of Nursing's 106-year history. It's harder to use when people have more sympathy for the keyworkers who were clapped every Thursday evening during Covid lockdown – health and care staff, shop workers, drivers and refuse collectors.

You can't pay the rent and feed a family on goodwill and saucepan banging.

Actually, unions exist for other people. They are based on the concept that many people campaigning for or against something will have more clout than one lone voice, particularly when dealing with mercenary and unscrupulous employers. And if the only power you have is your labour, then you'd be daft not to use that power by withdrawing your labour if that is the only option left to you.

Everyone in the UK has the right to join a trade union. You may have an employer who tries to stop you, but ultimately it is nothing to do with them whether you do, or, indeed, which union you join. Obviously it makes sense to belong to one that's relevant to your particular trade or profession. If you work in banking, for instance, it's not a terribly good idea to try and join NACODS, the National Association of Colliery Overmen, Deputies and Shotfirers.

Many of the highly specialised and rather quaint unions of the past have disappeared along with the trades they represented. For many years the Jewish Bakers' Union was a particular favourite of left-wing Trivial Pursuits players, with its eleven members making it the smallest union in the country – not even a baker's dozen.

We have bade farewell to the Associated Chiropodists and Podiatrists Union, to the Church and Oswaldwhistle Power-Loom Overlookers Society, to the Ice Hockey Players Association (Great Britain), the Society of Registration

Officers (Births, Deaths and Marriages) and the Union of Federation of Employed Door Supervisors and Security.

Most defunct unions become part of a larger one, although with a less romantic name. So anyone who enjoys working with feet can now belong to the new Society of Chiropractors and Podiatrists (which must have dropped the word union from its title to appear more upmarket), while bouncers can join the Security Industry Federation.

The passing of some great unions is understandably mourned by labour movement sentimentalists. Those who affectionately remember the great years of union power find it hard to believe that the Transport and General Workers' Union is no more. It merged with Amicus to create Unite. Amicus itself was the result of a merger between the AEEU (Amalgamated Engineering and Electrical Union) and the MSF (Manufacturing Science and Finance). But, as jobs have changed, or vanished completely, there's an argument that broader-based unions such as Unite or the GMB have more clout for the hundreds of thousands of members they represent, from Uber drivers to shop workers, ambulance crews, local government officers and farm food processors.

In 2022, around six million people in the UK were union members, working in every trade and profession from nurses and engineers to footballers and sheep shearers. That is about one in six of everyone who works. Although it's less than half of what it was in the 1970s, part of that is due to the changes in working life, but also because in those days, you couldn't get a job unless you joined a union. This was the closed shop which did a lot to boost union membership. – if you didn't join, you didn't work. It also made the unions extremely powerful, particularly in manufacturing and heavy industry, but in many other industries, including the media and the arts.

The Tories, employers and right-wingers everywhere saw this as a great plot. They argued that the unions were bullies forcing people to join so they could work and use their membership fees to support the Labour Party, which they did all they could to dominate. Opponents argued that it was a take-over of the government and the country by the back door.

Yet there was another side to this which you never read about in the papers. If you were one of the millions of people who felt disenfranchised by the control the establishment had over every part of the country, it didn't seem too bad that people who represented you were in there fighting on your behalf, however dirtily.

Of course, in reality, it was never like this. The unions never achieved the control their hysterical critics claimed they had and, anyway, there was rarely any indication that they had any positive influence on the Labour Party, let alone the government. At times, however, they had a major negative influence that kept Labour firmly out of power.

Eventually, in the early 1990s and after a series of laws that removed many of the powers of the unions, the closed shop was made illegal by Margaret Thatcher. Since then, there have been more and more restrictions on trades unions which have severely reduced their power.

Successive governments have restricted the right to picket and prevented unions bringing their members out in support of other unions. They also required at least 50 per cent of members to vote in ballots for strike action and those ballots are postal, even though, in 2022, members of the Conservative Party could vote electronically for a new leader and impose a Prime Minister on the rest of us.

So, organising industrial action takes time and money, which makes the gradual increase in union membership and the willingness to strike even more significant. Nurses, doctors, teachers, railway staff, bus drivers, council and postal workers, passport office staff and driving test examiners have all been part of the resurgence of industrial action since Covid.

When people talk about the death of the manufacturing industry, it's as though a sepia tint falls over Britain and we are transported to a Hovis-style ad where hundreds of cheery factory workers head off on their bikes to the allotments after a hard day making something.

In the late 1970s, manufacturing provided jobs for over 25 per cent of the UK's workforce and accounted for 30 per cent of our Gross Domestic Product. Today, it's less than 10 per cent of total UK economic output accounting for just 8 per cent of employment.

Ships, computer chips, planes, cars, tractors, machinery, furniture, pottery, cotton and steel can all be produced somewhere else in the world for less money.

Those former cotton mills, potteries and dockyards are

more likely to be part of the 'creative quarters' which have proved so valuable to the regeneration of towns and cities. Tin mines and goods sheds have become restaurants, while buildings that once housed great engines and hundreds of workers are now museums, where you can experience the discomfort of hard physical labour for a few minutes before going to the gift shop.

This different sort of industrial revolution, coupled with globalisation, has changed the way we work, buy and sell. Such huge changes left their mark on communities where once, virtually everyone worked for one employer, whether that was a shipyard, coal mine or food processing plant.

Even the most powerful and organised unions lost the battle to preserve traditional manufacturing jobs as the global tide of cheap labour and 24/7 communications swept away old jobs, leaving millions of workers high and dry. There are many who would argue that trade unions let their members down by failing to recognise that change was inevitable and, with that, different working conditions, different skills and different challenges were inevitable, too. The largely manual labour force from old-style manufacturing was ill-equipped to adapt and was simply elbowed out of the way by highly skilled people who could do the same job in another country, or here, for lower wages, without becoming involved in disruptive industrial action.

We wanted, and got, higher wages to enjoy the many pleasures of life which opened up to us: foreign holidays, cars, new furniture for our own homes, eating out regularly and lots of lovely cheap clothes. So, more and more employers decided that British workers could enjoy what they wanted, but that the work they had been doing would go to people who were content to rub along on a far more basic lifestyle in other countries.

British manufacturing adapted by playing to its strengths of design, technology, creativity, innovation and service, but that rarely involved actually making anything in the traditional sense. Factories and heavy industries are largely consigned to history, replaced by Amazon warehouses, tech innovation hubs and co-working spaces. Online shopping and home deliveries have made many high streets and retail outlets redundant. Brexit has created confusion and uncertainty, the two things that businesses hate most, which mean that investment is harder to come by. While there's optimism that new 'green' technologies might create new opportunities and jobs, it's more likely to be the entrepreneur who has made millions by developing a towelling robe for swimmers (and smug types who wear them to the shops so we all know they've embraced 'wild swimming') or created niche markets in the fine foods and luxury goods sectors, or services we didn't know we needed, who are going to be the employers of the future.

As industry has diversified, so too have workers' demands and concerns. Grievances against employers are now as likely to be about bullying, discrimination and stress than unreasonable hours or dangerous machinery. Health and safety laws, the minimum wage, equality legislation and European rules have, to a large extent, resolved many of the issues that topped the unions' campaign agenda for years.

Most of us who work do so in relatively safe and clean environments. We are entitled to paid holidays and sick pay, parental leave and a minimum wage and we can't be discriminated against because of the colour of our skin, our gender, age, faith or disability.

On just about every count we are hugely better off than the majority of the people who now produce the things we buy. The cheap clothes we purchase on the high street may be made by children in sweatshops thousands of miles away. Those out-of-season green beans and strawberries we take for granted have most likely been grown and harvested by African or South American farmers earning a pittance. And don't even think about avocados. Countless millions who harvest them receive subsistence-level wages or below, work in appalling conditions with virtually no time off and can be fired at whim.

The reason we are so much better off isn't because British employers are capitalistic saints, or enlightened bosses who skip among their workers distributing fat pay packets and begging them to work shorter hours and take longer holidays. It is because of the men and women who campaigned, marched, fought, suffered and even died to get better working conditions.

Despite the improvements for British workers over the past century, we work some of the longest hours in Europe, have far less job security in the current global economic climate and are increasingly worried about when we can retire and what we'll live on when we do. The pressure to put more hours in, be constantly available on phone or email and to learn new skills, meet targets, increase profit margins and cope with changes at work is enormous – in both the public and private sectors.

So here is this confusing conundrum. Unions have achieved a huge amount, and there is still a lot more to do. Yet they remain despised by large sections of the population and the press, who are convinced that union leaders are rabid, dangerous socialists who live a life of luxury on salaries many times that of their members and are determined to end our way of life.

Only you can decide. But if you go through your entire working life without ever needing support or advice, never experience bullying, discrimination or poor conditions, you'll be pretty unique.

CHAPTER 35

POLITICAL SCANDALS – THE OLD, OLD STORY

Sex, lies, drugs, money and corruption. All of these, and more, have been swirling around Westminster for ever. And, in some ways, that's not surprising if you stick hundreds of people together in a place that's full of strange rules, rituals and subsidised bars. MPs and peers, special advisers and journalists spend most of their working week in a place more like Hogwarts than a normal office, working silly hours, away from normal life and treated as though they're special.

The whole place thrives on gossip and rumour: who's in favour, who's going to be sacked and who knows more than the next person. But, outside, in the real world, the public and the media are far less willing to turn a blind eye to the kind of behaviour that would be totally unacceptable outside Parliament, as MPs discover when scandalous goings-on in and around the Palace of Westminster are revealed by the terrier-like investigations of some journalists.

In 2009, after painstaking work, legal challenges and

sheer determination, the *Daily Telegraph* exposed the MPs' expenses scandal. Many claimed for second homes, some were claiming for second homes they didn't need, some paid members of their families and a nanny out of public funds, some claimed for utility bills, for a duck house, porn videos and the cost of cleaning out the moat of a country estate. One MP even claimed he'd forgotten he'd paid off his mortgage, which is why he was still claiming the second-home allowance. There was, not surprisingly, public outrage, apologies from the Prime Minister and promises to overhaul the system. Most errant MPs agreed to pay back the money and a new expenses watchdog was set up, the Independent Parliamentary Standards Authority (IPSA), but there are still very big questions over what and how MPs and peers can spend their money on. There is nothing to stop any of them paying a consultant to help with their 'image' and members of the House of Lords can claim more than £300 a day for simply turning up, regardless of whether they contribute to proceedings. They can claim this even for attending an online, 'virtual' meeting. Some MPs also have lucrative second jobs and some have been caught out offering their services for huge fees to companies wanting access to ministers.

None of this is particularly new. In the 1840s, Disraeli, who was notoriously bad with money, borrowed the equivalent of what would now be almost £4 million to buy himself a country home, and there is no evidence that he ever paid the money back. Lloyd George openly had a mistress and sold peerages to raise money. Anthony Eden was addicted to amphetamines and Harold Wilson became entangled with shady businessmen. Liberal Democrat leader Paddy Ashdown's ratings went up when he admitted having a brief affair with his secretary and was forever known as 'Paddy Pantsdown', thanks to the *Sun* headline that followed his confession. Peter, now Lord, Mandelson had to resign because of questions about a loan to buy a swanky house in Notting Hill. Tory Minister David Mellor was caught with his trousers down and a model who claimed he wore a Chelsea FC strip while he sucked her toes.

But it was the Profumo Affair that really changed the way people saw politicians and brought the House of Cards tumbling down. It was 1961, the height of the Cold War, and it involved the Minister for War, a country house, a Russian agent and a young model. John Profumo had a fling with Christine Keeler, twenty-seven years his junior, the affair beginning at a party at Cliveden, the country mansion then owned by Viscount Astor. Keeler, whose image is forever etched in a famous black-and-white photo of her naked, astride a chair, was also involved with a Russian agent. The scandal rocked the British establishment, brought down the government and the gloves were off for the press. People stopped thinking that politicians were special and felt they could say so in public. Deference was dead; it was OK to poke fun at politicians and the age of satire began.

And there's more...

Take a party leader and a male model walking a Great Dane called Rinka. The dog gets shot by a man called Andrew

Netwon. In 1975, Jeremy Thorpe was the leader of the Liberal Party, Norman Scott was a male model and there were rumours that the pair had been lovers. Not only would this have been devastating for Thorpe's political career, as homosexuality was illegal then, but Thorpe was accused of arranging for Newton to kill Scott but was acquitted of attempted murder at the Old Bailey, though hardly anyone thought he was innocent.

One year earlier, a pile of clothes was found on a Miami beach with no sign of their owner, Labour Minister and MP John Stonehouse. Most people assumed he had drowned. The FBI thought he might have been the victim of a mafia hit and dug up a nearby car park. His death was even marked by a minute's silence in the Commons. But almost six weeks later, he was discovered alive and well, living in Australia with his secretary. Stonehouse had set up a string of dodgy companies to supplement his MP's salary and they were under investigation. His business was in ruins so he had faked his own death, taking the name of a dead constituent to begin his new life. The police who nabbed him thought they had got the missing peer Lord Lucan, but that's another story. Stonehouse was extradited and resumed his duties as a Labour MP while on remand in Brixton Prison before properly resigning in 1976, and ended up with a seven-year prison sentence.

Jeffrey Archer was a leading figure in the Conservative Party, famous for lavish parties and charity auctions and the author of surprisingly popular books. Then, in 1986, the *Daily Star* ran a story saying he had not only slept with a prostitute, Monica Coghlan, but paid her hush money. Archer completely denied the story, sued for libel and won, collecting a large sum in damages. Fourteen years later, it was revealed that the *Star*'s story was correct and that Archer had lied in court. He was found guilty of perjury and perverting the course of justice and sentenced to four years in prison, of which he served two, during which time he wrote and later published three volumes of prison diaries. Oddly, that time gets but a passing mention on his website.

Jonathan Aitken, another Tory MP, also went to prison for perjury. He had lied in court when he sued *The Guardian* over a story they ran about him staying at the Paris Ritz as a guest of a Saudi Arabian businessman, which, as Aitken was a government minister at the time, would have been a serious breach of parliamentary protocol. Aitken, a former journalist, declared at the time: 'If it falls to me to start a fight to cut out the cancer of bent and twisted journalism in our country with the simple sword of truth and the trusty shield of British fair play, so be it. I am ready for the fight.' The sword was as bent as his denial and he was jailed for eighteen months in 1999. Since his release, he has campaigned for the rights of prisoners and ex-offenders and is now an ordained prison chaplain.

Jared O'Mara is a convicted fraudster and former Labour MP for Sheffield Hallam. In 2017 he unexpectedly won the seat from former Liberal Democrat leader and Deputy Prime Minister, Nick Clegg, but stood down just two years later and in 2023 was found guilty of six counts of fraud and sentenced to four years in prison.

CHAPTER 36

NO, MINISTER – THE CIVIL SERVICE

If you thought no occupation had as short a lifespan as a football manager, who seem to change almost as often as the players' boots, think again.

When Rachel Maclean was announced as the new Housing Minister in February 2023, she became the fifteenth since the Tories came to power and the fifth to hold the post in the previous twelve months. (Still, beat the record of Lee Rowley, who held the position for just seven weeks, apparently leaving no trace.)

The UK has had eleven Culture Secretaries, eleven Justice Secretaries and ten Environment Secretaries since 2010, and in the four years after 2019, nearly half of all senior Cabinet posts have had as many people in the role as there were in the previous nine years. One MP, Grant Shapps, has had five Cabinet posts in a year – one, as Home Secretary, for less than a week. This is the league table of government roundabouts:

- Chancellor: 5

- Home Secretary: 4
- Housing Secretary: 5
- Health Secretary: 5
- Business Secretary: 6
- Education Secretary: 6
- Northern Ireland Secretary: 5

And that is just the top level, the Secretaries of State who are meant to be in charge of huge government departments, making decisions and policies that have an impact on us all. Lower down the government food chain, junior ministers have been in, out, changed departments and disappeared to the back benches. Oh, and some departments have been merged, renamed or scrapped. It's a wonder that anything keeps working at all and hardly surprising when there are glitches, never mind the cost of new name badges every five minutes.

The reason the country doesn't just collapse with all this chopping and changing is thanks to the civil service, which by and large keeps things functioning by putting the policy programme of the elected government into practice. Civil servants deal with everything from pensions to passports, tax benefits, driving licences, schools and prisons and thousands of other cogs in the machinery of government. They have to be politically neutral but dedicated to ministers' priorities, which of course can change overnight when there's a reshuffle. Civil servants are not allowed to stand for election as MPs, are subject to the Official Secrets Act and have restrictions on their contact with lobbyists.

Like most relationships, the one between politicians and civil servants is far from perfect and the men and women of Whitehall are often portrayed as lazy penpushers, resistant to change while happy to put red tape and bureaucracy in the way of progress. That is rather unfair, particularly as they are not allowed to defend themselves in public or act according to their personal beliefs, even when they are constantly under attack from ministers and MPs, some of whom, such as Michael Gove, have publicly called them 'The Blob', a mass of pathetic, left-leaning, Remain-supporting functionaries trying to block the government's agenda. Obviously, you would be thrilled about going into work every day knowing that's what your boss thought of you.

There are natural tensions between politicians, who decide policies, and the people who have to make those policies work. Sometimes politicians who want to be seen to be 'doing something' come up with ideas designed to get a favourable headline without any thought about whether those ideas would actually work. They rarely welcome anyone suggesting that their brilliant idea is flawed or just plain bonkers, but it's also true that politicians with energy, dynamism and determination can be frustrated by the glacial pace of the civil service. This is where special advisers or SPADS come in. Because they work directly for ministers, they are political appointments and are often very ambitious, bright, young people who think they know better than seasoned civil servants or foul-mouthed bullies like the character Malcolm Tucker in the TV satire *The Thick of It*. The originally awkward relationship has now become a ménage à trois and even more tricky.

Successive governments frustrated by the civil service's slow pace of delivery have tried to change the way that it works. The idea of adopting an American system where senior civil servants would be political appointments as opposed to being neutral was abandoned. On the other hand, the success of the Covid vaccine roll-out is attributed to bringing in an outsider, Kate Bingham, who chaired the government's Vaccine Taskforce and pulled various strands together at impressive speed to deliver what she was asked to do in unprecedented circumstances. Although bringing in the Tory peer Dido Harding to run the test-and-trace system was an unmitigated, very expensive disaster (£37 billion wasted for no results).

The civil service is often criticised for lacking specialists like data scientists and techno-savvy people who could earn far more and further their careers more quickly in the private sector. Then there are the people who have been in the job too long and are resistant to change, resigned to, and perhaps wearied by, the constant churn of ministers and their initiatives. The civil service is very hierarchical, which breeds a 'group-think' culture, making it difficult for outsiders to challenge practices and processes.

However, very few MPs, never mind ministers, have the breadth of managerial experience that heading a large government department needs. Most of them wouldn't last a day outside the unreal world of Westminster or Whitehall and their default position is often to blame officials who are not allowed to put their side of the argument.

Government and the way our country is run are complex. Competing demands for stability while also being agile and flexible were demonstrated all too clearly during the pandemic. While the vaccine roll-out was hailed as a great success, multi-million-pound contracts were awarded to companies that were clearly unsuitable, while firms who could have provided stuff that worked like masks and gowns never got a look-in. Eat Out to Help Out cost a fortune and probably spread the virus anyway, but we would never have found out through Test and Trace anyway, which did neither.

Political turmoil in the UK global events and instability have laid bare the need for reform in the way that the government and civil service work together. Perhaps a starting point might be for incoming ministers to think of the word 'civil' and build mutual respect within teams by encouraging discussion, debate and even dissent. Any good manager will tell you, you get more out of people by being … well, civil.

CHAPTER 37

LOCAL GOVERNMENT

You might think that what local councils do is boring. Really? You wouldn't think it was boing if your bins weren't emptied, your streets were littered, rats ran loose in the streets, your leisure centre was sold off, your schools weren't teaching children properly, there weren't carers for the elderly or social workers to look after the disabled or if planning control was so useless that new houses were built near your home.

These are all functions and duties of local government and they have more impact on the lives of most people than the actions of the government in Westminster.

Councils can fine you for not clearing up dog mess, drinking alcohol or parking in the wrong place, and if you're homeless, it will be the local authority that might put you on a waiting list. Good luck with that one. More on housing – or lack of – elsewhere.

Local government decides what time pubs, clubs and restaurants can open and close, where and when bus services run, who gets school places and free travel on public transport. It looks after street lighting and social care for adults and children, along with environmental health, which might sound boring but means kitchens in restaurants, cafés and other food outlets aren't going to give you food poisoning.

Depending on where you live, you might have a town or borough council, as well as a county council, parish council or metropolitan district. You might even have an elected mayor as well as elected councillors, each representing a 'ward', which is the heart of a local area.

There are different systems of local government around the country but they all work on the principle of elected councillors working with council officers who are the paid local civil service. Far from being boring, your local council is vital to your everyday life.

To add spice to the mix, the local council will often be of a different political persuasion to the MP, and in some areas, councillors from different political parties work together more harmoniously than their national colleagues.

FUNDING

Local councils get money from central government and raise more from council tax, business rates, parking charges and fines for littering and graffiti. Most of the money they get is not frittered away but is spent on education and social services.

Because the biggest chunk of funding comes from central

government, when that is cut, as it has been since 2010, it means councils have to cut services like libraries and community centres. It also means councils have sold off buildings and land they owned or outsourced services like leisure centres to private companies which then pushed up prices. It is a cynical ploy by central government to slash grants to councils in the hope that people will blame their local councils for services being slashed,

Some desperate councils have tried to play the market and raise money in what have turned out to be terrible deals with developers or over-ambitious plans. Croydon, Woking, Birmingham and Nottingham councils have effectively declared bankruptcy and local government leaders expect more will follow.

Because councils are desperate for money, they can feel under pressure to do deals with housing and other developers that aren't always best for the local area in the long term. Once a library or community centre is closed, it's hard to get it back. Once playing fields have been sold off and built on, they are gone for ever. So, councils aren't able to plan for the future and, because services are run on such tight margins, when something like Covid comes along, or an unexpected and serious event like extreme weather, they haven't got the resources or wiggle-room to cope.

A lot of the money they might get from central government is awarded by a sort of competition, where councils have to apply for grants, which means a council that has the people and time to produce a good application has more chance of success than a council that's already stretched. If they do get extra funding, central government often puts restrictions on how that money is used, which rather dilutes the idea of local people being able to decide what's best for their area.

Some might say it's a coincidence, others might say it's bribery, but either way, councils can't plan ahead if the only way to win a share of funding from national government is through a begging-bowl competition. Research by *The Guardian* in 2023 found that 'voters in Tory seats got £19.47 more a head than those in similarly deprived non-Conservative constituencies from the Levelling Up fund. Even the National Audit Office says that, in many cases, areas that benefitted most from central government funds for improving town centres were 'disproportionately drawn from marginal Conservative-held constituencies and the scheme might therefore benefit the Conservatives in any future election'. And that's another reason you could argue why our current voting system is in need of reform, because those marginal seats can determine the next government.

SENDING A MESSAGE TO WESTMINSTER

When something is happening on our doorsteps that we, the public, don't like, we are like sleeping dragons suddenly roused into action. If it's a big issue, the local MP may get involved too and raise the matter with government ministers or in the House of Commons. MPs clinging on to their seat might suddenly realise that people do care about recycling, better rural bus services and access to evening classes. Those same MPs can warn their colleagues at Westminster that this is a big local issue and might cost them an MP at the next election, so they need to take notice.

Well-organised local campaigns can have a huge impact on local councils, as demonstrated in Plymouth in the spring of 2023. The felling of 119 trees in Plymouth city centre under cover of darkness led to public protests, children's artwork being removed, celebrities getting involved, a council leader, forced to resign and a humiliating defeat for the council in court. Followed by a humiliating defeat for the controlling Tories at the next council election a few weeks later and Labour taking control of Plymouth council.

LOCAL INFLUENCE

In any town, city or village there are usually local people who influence decisions about schools, hospitals, transport, business and the arts. They might be elected school governors, members of a patient or health campaign group, local business people, faith leaders or people campaigning for safer cycling or to stop sewage being dumped in our seas and rivers.

Charities, trade unions, church and other community groups took up a lot of the slack during Covid that would have been previously left to the local council. That local knowledge and connection provided food banks, transport, shopping and other support to vulnerable people and was quicker and more agile in being able to respond.

Britain is full of people involved in things that are important to them, their families and their local area. Although few of them would call themselves politicians, they all play a huge part in our democracy and in shaping the places we live, work, study and play in.

A PATH TO POWER

Many politicians begin their careers in local government and the Liberal Democrats and Greens have more representation at local level than nationally. In fact, 'doorstep' political campaigning has helped those two parties gain a power base that is not reflected at Westminster, which takes us back to the question of proportional representation. Again.

If it wasn't for the Liberal Democrats and Greens banging on about doorstep recycling years ago and being laughed at by the other parties, we probably wouldn't have as much recycling as we do, and even that varies from one local council to the other.

FACTS

Local councils provide many services. They must provide some of these by law, known as statutory services, such as education, which are heavily controlled by central government. Other services are optional or discretionary services, such as pest removal.

LOCAL GOVERNMENT

- Education – providing schools, transport to get children to and from school and opportunities for adult learning;
- Housing – finding accommodation for people in need and maintaining social housing;
- Social services – caring for and protecting children, older and disabled people;
- Highways and transport, including maintaining roads and managing traffic flow;
- Waste management, including collecting rubbish and recycling;
- Leisure and cultural services – providing libraries, leisure services and arts venues;
- Consumer protection, such as enforcing trading standards and licensing taxis;
- Environmental health and services, such as making sure that the food provided in pubs and restaurants is safe to eat, and controlling local pollution;
- Planning, including managing local development and making sure buildings are safe;
- Economic development – attracting new businesses and encouraging tourism;
- Emergency planning for things like floods and terrorist attacks.

- In 2021, the Isles of Scilly Council was the smallest local authority by population, with 2,100 people.

- In 2021, Kent County Council was the largest local authority by population, with 1,578,500 people.
- In 2022, 40 per cent of local councillors were retired and only 32 per cent – less than a third – were in full- or part-time employment.
- In 2022, 61 per cent of councillors held other voluntary or unpaid positions, such as school governorships.
- In 2022, 59.1 per cent of councillors were male.
- The average age of councillors in 2022 was 60; 16 per cent were aged under 45 and 42 per cent were aged 65 or over.
- In 2022, 92 per cent described their ethnic background as white.
- In 2022, 84.1 per cent described their sexual orientation as heterosexual or straight, 4.2 per cent as gay or lesbian and 2.2 per cent as bisexual.

CHAPTER 38

GRENFELL

It started on a summer night with an electrical fault in a fridge. The sort of thing that can happen in any home and rarely has serious consequences, But this time it led to seventy-two people dying and more than seventy being injured. It was the worst fire in the UK since the Second World War and the reason it was so deadly was because building safety regulations had been ignored.

The fire was in Grenfell Tower, a 24-storey block of flats in North Kensington, West London. It broke out shortly after midnight on 14 June 2017 on the fourth floor – which meant that there were people on twenty floors above who had to get out when the blaze took hold. Miraculously, 223 escaped. Hundreds of firefighters fought for sixty hours to bring the fire under control. The blackened husk of the building was left as a terrible monument.

By the time the smouldering remains had stopped smoking, the big question was already being asked: HOW could this have happened? It was quickly realised that the flames had spread up the outside of the building by racing up the cladding which had been fixed on to Grenfell. It was with horror that it was learned that the cladding was made from dangerously combustible aluminium, which created an air gap with the building's external insulation so that the flames sped up the tower.

The finger of blame was pointed firmly at Kensington and Chelsea Council and its housing body, but there was also criticism of many other organisations. Even the fire brigade did not escape censure – they had told residents trapped in their flats that they should not try to escape: advice which led to many of them being burned alive. This awful tragedy was the result of a series of blunders and failures, especially cuts to council funding, which meant building inspections were not properly carried out, failures by the companies which built Grenfell and those that sold the cladding and other materials, and government deregulation policies, which led to an inadequate number of checks being carried out on a building in which hundreds of people, including children and the elderly, were living.

Parliament ordered a review of building regulations and fire safety, while other tower blocks with similar cladding were investigated. The conclusion was that this cladding should be replaced in scores of other blocks, but there was then a standoff between councils, builders and manufacturers over who should pay for this work, so it is proceeding tortuously slowly, leaving thousands of people still living in potentially lethal homes.

GRENFELL

Although 900 of those involved in the Grenfell disaster have received payments from various manufacturers and building firms, no individual or company has been charged with any criminal offence. We are told that investigations are continuing. Don't hold your breath.

CHAPTER 39

WHAT WE'VE LOST

Great Britain deserved to be called 'Great' for more reasons than being master of the world's seas and ruling a globe-spanning empire. We were admired for our parliamentary system of government, our police force, our courts and justice system, our welfare state and, particularly, our National Health Service, as well as our tolerance.

While the British Empire and our mastery of the waves were never going to last for ever, there was a belief that all those other marks of civilisation would not only survive, but expand. How naïve we were. As we hope this book has shown, the past few years have seen several of the advances made in the previous century reversed or, at best, watered down.

The most basic hallmark of a democracy is that everyone above a certain age should have the vote. Note that it is known as *the* vote, not *a* vote, because it is so important. Once you reach the age of eighteen – and there can be a discussion about whether that should be lowered – you have the absolute right to turn up at a polling station on election day and play your part in deciding who should represent you in the nation's Parliament, who will form the government or who will run your local council.

This is not a right that was graciously granted by the King centuries ago. In fact, it was refused for a very long time and even then was grudgingly rolled out slowly. It had to be fought for. From the time that 'ordinary people' (as opposed to Lords alone) were allowed to get involved in choosing their Member of Parliament, it was a long, slow struggle before universal franchise was achieved and the people who ran the country conceded that even women could have the vote.

Job done. Or was it? Ninety-four years after every adult had finally been given the vote, the government passed a law making it harder to exercise it. They decreed that no one would be allowed to assume this basic right unless they could show some form of identification. The pretence for introducing this was that it would prevent anyone turning up at the polling station and pretending to be someone else, but how widespread was this abuse? At the previous election the number of people found to be doing this was one. Yes, just one. Out of an electorate of 46.5 million registered parliamentary electors (and 2 million more who could vote in local elections), only one person committed this offence, yet this was used as an excuse to interfere with one of the most fundamental rights of every British citizen.

As there clearly wasn't a genuine problem with personation

(which is what pretending to be someone else is called legally), what was the government up to? The clue is in the people most likely to not have the forms of identification needed and so not be able to vote. While you could show a pensioner's bus pass and get into the polling booth, a student's or young person's pass was not acceptable. And as old people are far more likely to vote Conservative, that makes it look as if the scheme is nothing but a Tory attempt to fiddle with the outcome of elections. This is known as gerrymandering, and you don't have to take our word for it. No less a person than the former Leader of the Commons, Sir Jacob Rees-Mogg, who had argued for the voting changes in Parliament, has said that is exactly what it is. The Electoral Reform Society, which had warned that 'this unnecessary policy would be a messy and expensive distraction, posing a real risk that genuine voters would lose their democratic right to vote', produced research after the first election in which it was used showing that 1,400 people had been turned away from polling stations. Their basic democratic right to vote had been undermined.

Another hard-won right is the one which allows workers to strike, which was only achieved by decades of struggle against hard-hearted bosses and unsympathetic governments. It was a great victory for the working class but the fundamental right to strike has been undermined over and over again since Mrs Thatcher set her hatchet man, Norman Tebbit, loose on trade union laws in the 1980s. Gradually, it became even harder for workers to withdraw their labour.

The latest assault is the government's bill to force some

employees to work despite them voting to strike, a move which will force people who have legally voted to strike to go to work and ignores key safeguards and undermines international labour standards. It gives ministers sweeping powers and allows them to ignore the usual management–worker route of negotiation. This is a throwback to the bad old days when bosses could simply tell their workers what to do – and no arguing back.

Another right under attack is the right to protest. It is a very long time since those who wanted to take a stand against oppressive or discriminatory laws or proposals were banned or attacked by the police or even the army. There have always been laws against public disorder or damage to property but simply protesting has been a treasured right. Of course there were always some who objected to protestors or who didn't like how their lives were disrupted by a march or protest, but it was widely accepted that the right to protest was fundamental to the British way of life. We looked down on those countries that banned any form of protest attacking those who dared to defy them and throwing them in jail.

It was like that in this country for many years, but the turning point came in 1819 at St Peter's Field, Manchester, when a crowd gathered to demand a reform of Parliament (at that time, only about half a million people had the vote out of a population of approximately 20 million adults, so you can see why they wanted reform). However, the government was less than sympathetic to their peaceful demand and ordered cavalry to charge them. Eighteen protestors were killed and as many as 700 wounded. The outcry was so strong that the government was stung into changing the law and meeting the demands of the Chartists, which was where the trades union movement sprung from. Since then, peaceful protest has been accepted as a proper part of a functioning British democracy. It has allowed marches of up to 1.5 million people, who paraded through London to object to the Iraq War, and 1.2 million who marched for a second referendum on the UK's membership of the EU (neither did any good; both Labour and Conservative governments ignored their demands).

It wasn't until the protests by Just Stop Oil began and disrupted traffic that the Tory government took the opportunity to rush through legislation that imposed stringent punishments on those who protested. Turning out to express your unhappiness at what you saw as policies which threatened the future of civilisation and the planet could see you bundled into the back of a police van, locked up and facing a lengthy term in jail. Bye-bye to the right to protest.

Another of the most fundamental and treasured rights of the British people is that anyone accused of an offence gets a fair hearing. If they are charged with a serious offence, there has been the right to trial by a jury of twelve ordinary people. This right has also been eroded in fact, to such an extent that a former law officer has claimed that the justice system has been the most damaged of any UK institution in recent years. The right to a jury trial had been guaranteed to anyone facing more than six months in prison, with their cases being heard in a Crown Court. In 2022, the law was changed to allow magistrates to hear cases that could result in a year's imprisonment. At the same time, magistrates were given new powers to decide cases purely on the paperwork, without the defendant appearing in court. Although these measures have since been reversed, this fundamental change to the justice system was slipped through with virtually no publicity or discussion.

These changes don't just affect the people of this country. They also change the way that the UK is viewed around the world. Britain has long been a byword for decency, compassion and justice – for doing the right thing – but we are losing that reputation which was built up over centuries.

Lowering the esteem in which this country is held also affects how Parliament is viewed. What was for so long seen as a model for other legislatures is now often viewed with derision. The misbehaviour and antics of many MPs and Ministers makes the UK look corrupt and unstable. Voting to leave the European Union was a move that was looked on with astonishment almost everywhere else. Boris Johnson was seen as a joke figure when he became Prime Minister, an opinion which his antics confirmed, and then he was replaced by Liz Truss, who only lasted for forty-nine days. On top of that, these two appointed so many people to the House of Lords that it now has more members than any legislature in the world, apart from China's National People's Congress, which has almost 3,000. Mind you, as China's population is twenty times larger than ours, if they had the same proportion of parliamentarians to population as we do, they would have 16,000 politicians in their Congress.

One other once-great British institution that is no longer what it was is the National Health Service. For seventy-five years it has given peace of mind and free treatment to the people of this country, a model of healthcare which all but the most right-wing governments with their fingers in the trough of private treatment marvel at. We still have superb doctors and nurses but the NHS has been deprived of the money it needs to keep up with a growing and ageing population, while hospitals built decades ago are crumbling into disrepair. The stark fact is that we spend less per head of population on health than other large, developed countries. There is not a lot for other nations to admire there now.

So here is the greatest challenge for future generations – to rebuild our nation and the institutions which made us so admired but which we are losing, and losing fast.

CHAPTER 40

WHAT NOW?

So if you look at what has been going on in this country, you will spot a pattern. More than one actually. The rich have got richer while most of us have not and the poor have got even poorer. Help has been targeted at older people while the young have had to suffer the repeated undermining of their lives now and in the future.

This is not to say life is cushy for the elderly. It isn't for millions and the UK continues to have one of the lowest state pensions in the developed world. However, a series of massive problems face young people including the nature and security of the work they can get, the life-long burden of paying back university tuition fees and the difficulties of getting a home of their own or even being able to afford a rented place.

There is a simple, if cynical, reason for this difference between how the young and old are treated. The elderly not only tend to vote, but a significant proportion of them vote Conservative while the young don't, and indeed far too many of them don't vote at all, a point we made at the beginning of this book but which can never be emphasised enough.

What's odd is that among the older generation are people who took to the streets, protested and even rioted against nuclear arms, apartheid, the Vietnam War, racial and sexual discrimination. They did it without social media and made their voices heard, not just in the UK but in the USA and Europe and helped shape the world in which we live. So where is that spirit of revolution and desire for change today? The commitment to standing up for people who don't have a voice, don't have a vote? The guts to call out the crooks, the con-artists and charlatans who have debased our democracy and our reputation as a country of fairness, tolerance and de-cency? Of course, none of those things has simply vanished but sometimes they're hard to find when so many people just shrug their shoulders and say all politicians are the same and voting makes no difference.

The answer to the question Why Vote? is obvious. If you don't, you will find politicians take the easy way out and do as little as they can get away with when it comes to help-ing younger people and the next generation. The threat to the entire planet from climate change is getting closer and frighteningly real. Russia, China and India are becoming more powerful and the world order is changing, presenting new challenges in cyber and traditional warfare, fake news and disinformation. Politicians of all parties have failed on so many levels to deal with crises in housing, the environment, health, immigration and education. Pantomime politics at

Westminster have taken centre stage for too long. Nobody's been concentrating on the unsexy stuff like making sure school buildings are safe, dealing with the backlog of asylum claims, ever-increasing NHS waiting lists, the pollution of our seas and rivers, unreliable and expensive public transport, prisons that aren't fit for purpose and shortages of key workers.

The solution is clear. Vote. The rest is up to you.